ELEVEN EUROPEAN MYSTICS

ELEVEN EUROPEAN MYSTICS

By
Rudolf Steiner

Translated from the German by Karl E. Zimmer

Introductory Comment by Paul M. Allen

RUDOLF STEINER PUBLICATIONS
151 North Moison Road
Blauvelt, New York 10913, U.S.A.
1971

Library of Congress Catalogue Card Number (60-15703)

Manufactured in the United States of America

CONTENTS

ABOUT THE AUTHOR, THE PEOPLE,
AND THE BACKGROUND OF THIS BOOK

SHORTLY BEFORE the beginning of the present century, Rudolf Steiner arrived in Berlin to assume the post of editor of the well-known *Magazin für Litteratur* which had been established by Joseph Lehmann in 1832, the year of Goethe's death. Steiner was well qualified for this position, having already edited and written commentary on the natural scientific writings of Goethe for the Kurschner and the Weimar Editions of Goethe's works, a task for which he had been originally recommended by the celebrated Goethe scholar, Karl Julius Schröer, under whom Steiner had studied at the University of Vienna. Steiner also had edited the works of Schopenhauer and Jean Paul Richter for the well-known Cotta *Library of World Literature* series. Steiner's work as a writer for various periodicals in Vienna, Weimar and Berlin included observations on current affairs, reviews of books and plays, and comment on scientific, social, and philosophical developments.

As an author in his own right, Steiner had already produced his *Grundlinien einer Erkenntnistheorie der Goetheschen Weltanschauung,* Theory of Knowledge in Goethe's Conception of the World, in 1886 at the age of twenty-five. In this book he revealed his comprehensive grasp of the deeper implications of Goethe's way of thinking. During his Weimar residence while working at the Goethe-Schiller Archives as a free collaborator on the Weimar Edition of Goethe, Steiner developed lines of thought which he later expressed in his *Goethes Weltanschauung,* Goethe's Conception of the World, published in 1897. These two works, together with his introductions and commentary on Goethe's scientific writings, established Steiner as one of the outstanding exponents of Goethe's methodology.

In 1891 Steiner received his Ph.D. at the University of Rostock. His thesis dealt with the scientific teaching of Fichte, and is evidence of Steiner's ability to evaluate the work of men whose influence has gone far to shape the thinking of the modern world. In somewhat enlarged form this thesis appeared under the title *Wahrheit und Wissenschaft,* Truth and Science, as the preface to Steiner's chief philosophical work, *Die Philosophie der Freiheit,* 1894. Later he suggested *The Philosophy of Spiritual Activity* as the title of the English translation of this book.

Steiner's contact with the circle of Friedrich Nietzsche led to his work in the Nietzsche Archives and Library. Out of the profound impression the ideas of Nietzsche made upon him, he wrote his *Friedrich Nietzsche, Ein Kämpfer gegen seine Zeit,* now published for the first time in English translation as *Friedrich Nietzsche, Fighter for Freedom,* as a part of the Centennial Edition of the Major Writings of Rudolf Steiner, 1861-1961.

With Steiner's arrival in Berlin, his lecturing activity which had begun years before in Vienna, and had been continued in Weimar, was extended and increased. Eventually this work was to occupy the major portion of his time, and was to take him on repeated lecture tours throughout Western Europe. These journeys extended from Norway, Sweden, and Finland in the north to Italy and Sicily in the south, and included several visits to the British Isles. From about the turn of the century until his death in 1925, Steiner gave well over 6,000 lectures before audiences of most diverse backgrounds and from every walk of life.

Steiner's written works, which eventually included over fifty titles, together with his extensive lecturing activity, brought him into contact with increasing numbers of people in many countries. The sheer physical and mental vigor required to carry on a life of such broad, constant activity is sufficient to mark him as one of the most creatively productive men of our time.

*

The present book, *Mysticism at the Dawn of the Modern Age,* is a fruit of Steiner's lecturing activity. The substance of it was contained in a series of lectures he gave in Berlin beginning just after Michaelmas in 1900, when he was thirty-nine. Steiner wrote later, "By means of the ideas of the mystics from Meister Eckhart to Jacob Boehme, I found expression for the spiritual perceptions which, in reality, I decided to set forth. I then summarized the series of lectures in the book, *Mysticism at the Dawn of the Modern Age*."

The term *mysticism,* as Steiner uses it in this book, is a further development of what Goethe indicated in his aphoristic description of mysticism in relation to poetry and philosophy. "Poetry," said Goethe, "points to the riddles of nature, and tries to solve them by means of the image. Philosophy directs itself to the riddles of reason, and attempts to solve them by means of the word. Mysticism considers the riddles of both nature and reason, and seeks to solve them through both word and image."

This book is significant in the life-work of Rudolf Steiner because it is a first result of his decision to speak out in a direction not immediately apparent in his earlier, more philosophical writings, mentioned above. Here— particularly in Steiner's Introduction—is to be found a vitally fundamental exposition of the science of the spirit, embracing the path of spiritual knowledge suited to the needs and capacities of modern men and women. This subject occupied Steiner increasingly during the whole of the first quarter of this present century, and to it he devoted his entire talents as lecturer and writer.

*

Rudolf Steiner indicated that the present book is not intended to be a history of mysticism. It deals with a problem that had occupied him for decades, and which today has become a cardinal concern of all mankind: the impact of modern scientific thinking upon the experiences of man's inner, spiritual life. In the conflict between reason and revelation which reached its climax in the nineteenth century, but which had its origins in much earlier times, Steiner saw the seed of a still greater conflict to come, a conflict which involves humanity's struggle against the sub-human in modern technical developments.

It is now generally realized that the impact of the atomic age challenges man's inner convictions, his spiritual striving, and ultimately his ability to live a truly satisfying life.

In this book Steiner tells how eleven men whose lives bridge the four centuries from the Gothic time to the mid-seventeenth century, solved the conflict between their inner spiritual perceptions and the world of individual freedom, invention, and discovery then coming to birth. He explains the positive contribution of their ideas to an understanding and preservation of the humanity of modern men and women in face of contemporary events.

In order that the reader may better appreciate Steiner's presentation of the leading thoughts of these men, a brief sketch of their times and their life stories is given in the following pages.

＊

The period covered by the lives of the men whose ideas are discussed in this book links such diverse personalities as Dante Alighieri, who expressed the strivings of the Age of Faith in his *Divina Commedia,* and George Fox, whose experience of the inner light established the spiritual path of the Society of Friends in a century of skepticism and growing materialism. Great changes in human thinking took place in these four hundred years. The world of chivalry and knighthood, of pious hermit and wandering minstrel, of religious pilgrimage and miracle play, so characteristic of the medieval time, gave way to the new learning, the humanism, the centralized governments, the scientific investigation, the expanding horizons, both physical and mental, of the Renaissance. And no single part of human life was untouched by the change. In the political, religious, social, intellectual spheres the Renaissance worked its wonders, and the dream of the Middle Ages awakened to the glorious colors of the dawn of a new world.

The transformation in men's minds included a break with their former way of looking at the earth beneath their feet, at their fellow-men, and at the blue vault arching over their heads. From a conception of nature that saw the animate in everything—even in stones—new systems of classification, ways of analysis, of explanation, based more and more upon the evidence of the physical senses, and less and less upon folk-lore and tradition, came into being. The new cosmopolitanism, the recovery of the art and philosophy of ancient Greece, the breaking up of old parties and practices in the social and political life led ultimately to man's growing consciousness of *himself,* and of his intrinsic worth as a being among other beings. The discovery of the shape of the earth, the rebirth of geographic learning lost in the dimness of forgotten ages, finally brought men to think of the possibility of worlds beyond this world, of whole solar systems beyond ours, and the word *infinite* began to assume a new importance. In the genius of language is revealed the momentous change that took place in these centuries. One need only recall that to the medieval mind the word *reality* referred exclusively to spiritual, heavenly things, to see how far-reaching was the change that occurred at the dawn of the modern world.

Today, when modern technical developments have extended their sphere of activity to include interstellar space, and space travel is regarded as a rapidly approaching accomplishment, one can recall that to men of the Middle Ages even the high places of the earth itself were regarded with reverence as dwelling-places of Divinity. Medieval man disliked even to approach high mountains, and to climb them would have required a daring inconceivable to him. As Ruskin said, "Men of the Middle Ages believed that mountains were agreeable things enough, so long as they were far away."

With the rise of the new thinking of the Renaissance, however, men began to lose their awe of high mountains, and one of the pioneer mountain climbers was Petrarch, the Italian poet. With his brother Gherado, Petrarch climbed Mount Ventroux, a six thousand foot peak near Avignon, on April 26, 1336. All seems to have gone well until at the summit Petrarch discovered that the very clouds of heaven were beneath his feet. Overcome with excitement not unmixed with concern, he took out of his pocket a copy of Augustine's writings he always carried with him. Opening the book at random his eye fell upon a sentence which struck through him like lightning, for it sternly warned man never to lift his head out of the dust of earth, but always to remember his entire subservience to his Maker. Deeply moved, Petrarch descended the mountain filled with secret shame that he had had the temerity to trespass upon a place denied man by the teaching of the Church Fathers.

As men of the Middle Ages believed the mountains to be sacred, so they also regarded the human body as something set apart as the dwelling-place of man's immortal soul. Therefore to them the anatomical studies practised by Renaissance investigators like Leonardo da Vinci would have seemed blasphemous in the highest degree.

As Renaissance man learned to take possession of the earth with his thinking, he reached out to embrace its far places physically as well. The age of discovery and exploration was followed by a period of conquest and colonization.

Parallel with the humanistic impulses of the Renaissance ran the current of the Reformation, with the accompanying strife and violence of the Counter-Reformation. Finally, as the four centuries covered by the lives of the men considered in this book drew to a close, strong national states emerged, with cultural, political, and social activities closely interrelated.

The year Meister Eckhart was born, Louis IX, known to posterity as Saint Louis of France, leader of the last Crusade, died. When Angelus Silesius died, the *Grand Monarque*, Louis XIV, destined to rule France for seventy-two years, was thirty-nine years of age, in the full strength of his manhood.

From the foregoing can be seen that the period covered by the lives of these men is the time when humanity, particularly in the Western world, evolved into a condition of consciousness in which the things of the sense world dominate all other considerations, in contrast to the preceding age, when the things of the spirit prevailed to such an extent that no sacrifice of earthly things was considered too great if, for example, it would enhance the miraculous, heaven-aspiring glory of a rising Gothic cathedral.

1.

In the year 1260 while Marco Polo was on his way to China, thus giving birth to new East-West relationships, and Niccolo Pisano was calling deathless beauty to life in his sculpture in Pisa, Johannes Eckhart was born in the little Thuringian village of Hochheim near Gotha, in Germany. His father was a steward in a knight's castle, hence Johannes' boyhood was passed in the midst of the then fading pageantry of medieval life.

Eckhart was born in the time of transition between the end of the Hohenstaufen rule and the beginning of the reign of the Austrian Hapsburgs in Germany. The one hundred and sixteen years of Hohenstaufen rule (1138-1254) was probably the most interesting period in medieval Germany, and its influence was still active during Eckhart's boyhood, though the last Hohenstaufen had died six years before Eckhart's birth.

This was an age of great contrasts. On the one hand were men of strong, vigorous mind, filled with love for all that the world contained of beauty and adventure. On the other were men whose character was equally strong, but whose lives were spent in a continual struggle of rejection of the world and all its gifts. These were the years when

these two opposed attitudes toward the world began a conflict which was to lead to the Renaissance in Germany, and
at last to the Reformation. Typical of the Hohenstaufen
rulers was Frederick II, considered the most brilliant of
all German kings. He was a lover of poetry, art, literature,
and was a most capable ruler as well. Crowned at Aix-la-
Chapelle in July, 1215, Frederick combined the traditional knightly ideals with worldly activity. The rule of the
Hohenstaufens corresponded with the golden age of the
German *Minnesinger,* and was a time of architectural development, which included many beautiful churches as
well as the famous castle of the Wartburg.

At about the age of fifteen, around the year 1275, Eckhart entered the Dominican monastery at Erfurt, where he
remained for nine years in preparation for the priesthood.
He completed his studies in the year that Philip IV, known
as "the Fair" began his fateful reign in France.

From Erfurt, Eckhart went to Cologne to take the *stu-
dium generale* at the Dominican institution where the
eminent scholastic, Albertus Magnus was a leading teacher
until his death in 1280. Through his instructors at Cologne, Eckhart came under the influence of Albertus Magnus' ideas, as well as those of Thomas Aquinas, whose
work had advanced Scholasticism to a place of first importance within the Dominican Order.

The year 1300 was famous as the Year of Jubilee pro-
claimed by Boniface VIII, whom Dante criticized by plac-
ing him in the Inferno during the Pope's lifetime. In this
same year Eckhart is mentioned as "Brother Eckhart, Prior
of Erfurt, Vicar of Thuringia" in Dominican records. He

was now in his fortieth year, and about this time he produced a little book which bears the charming title, *Daz sint die rede der unterscheidunge, die der Vicarius von Düringen, der prior von Erfort, bruoder Eckehart predier ordens mit solichen kinden hete, diu in dirṛe rede frâgten vil dinges, dô sie sâzen in collationibus mit einander,* These are the Instructions which the Vicar of Thuringia, Prior of Erfurt, Brother Eckhart of the Preaching Order, gave for those of his flock who asked him about many things as they sat together at the evening meal.

At this time Eckhart was sent to one of the colleges in Paris, where he frequently entered into disputation with Franciscans in defense of Dominican points of view in theology. In his disputations he had to defend the writings of Thomas Aquinas and Albertus Magnus against any charges of heresy which the Franciscans chose to bring forward against them.

Thirteenth century Paris was a place of great attraction for scholars, and was the center of European cultural life. Over one hundred fifty years before, Pierre Abélard had written of his intense desire to visit Paris, the city where logical argumentation, beloved by the medieval scholarly mind, had been raised to the level of a fine art. John of Salisbury, Bishop of Chartres, eminent as a humanist long before the Renaissance, the secretary and counsellor of Thomas Becket of Canterbury, whose assassination he witnessed and whose life he recorded, loved Paris for its generous supply of food, the gaiety of its inhabitants, their appreciation of culture and religion, and the atmosphere of scholarship he found there. He summed up his feelings about Paris in the exclamation, "Indeed the Lord is in this place, and I did not know it!"

Years later Eckhart described his Paris activities in terms which perhaps explain why the Franciscans cherished no particular liking for him. With regard to his disputations with the Franciscans, Eckhart said, "When I preached at Paris, I said—and I dare repeat it now—that with all their learning the men of Paris are not able to conceive that God is in the very least of creatures—even in a fly!"

Words like these help one to understand Eckhart's popularity with the public of his time. For above all, Eckhart wished to reach the man in the street, the humble peasant, the shepherd from the mountains, the charcoal burner from the forest, the simplest of the simple, rather than the scholar in the cloister. Therefore he used colloquial German in all his writings and discourses rather than the usual theological Latin. Thus the German language was enhanced by the writings of this Dominican, just as the Italian language was enriched by his contemporary, Dante Alighieri.

Eckhart was always conscious of his indebtedness to the other great Dominicans who had preceded him, and although he did not follow their learned forms in his sermons and books, he never failed to recognize their superiority in learning. For example, his frequent quotations in his oral and written discourse were invariably introduced by the words, "A Master says," and the "Master" almost always meant Thomas Aquinas, whom he looked upon as a spiritual father. Though his genius for adapting learned, subtle arguments to simple, aphoristic form resulted in his being understood by the every-day mind, nevertheless this ultimately led to the condemnation of his teaching as heretical.

In 1302, the year after the famous Duns Scotus became professor of theology at Oxford, Eckhart received the Licentiate and Master's degree from the University of Paris. Ever since then he has been known as Meister Eckhart.

At this time Boniface VIII, who had been informed of the brilliant preaching of this Thuringian Dominican, invited Eckhart to Rome to defend the cause of the papacy against the attacks of the French king, Philip the Fair, which were soon to result in the "Babylonian Captivity" of the Popes at Avignon.

In 1304, the year of the birth of Petrarch, Eckhart was appointed provincial of the Dominicans for Saxony. Three years later he was appointed vicar-general for Bohemia, at the moment the arrest and terrible persecution of the Order of the Knights Templar began in France under the direction of Philip the Fair, and with the passive agreement of the French-born Pope, Clement V, who in the meanwhile had succeeded Boniface VIII in the papacy.

This was a busy period in the life of Meister Eckhart. His burden of administrative work in the service of the Church and of his Order was increased by his activity as a writer. At this time he composed one of his best-known works, *Das Büch der Göttlichen Tröstung,* The Book of Divine Comfort, supposedly written to bring consolation to Agnes, daughter of the King of Hungary, whose mother and sister-in-law died and whose father was murdered— all within the space of a few years.

The Book of Divine Comfort opens with an enumeration of the three kinds of tribulation Eckhart conceives may happen to one: damage to external goods, to friends near one, to oneself, bringing "disgrace, privation, physical suffering, and mental anguish" in their train. As "comfort" in the midst of such tribulation, Eckhart sets forth "certain doctrines" from which he derives "thirty teachings, any one of which should be enough to comfort." Whether the suffering of the Queen of Hungary was assuaged by Eckhart's effort in her behalf is not known, but the book brought Eckhart himself considerable tribulation, for it is his one work most strenuously attacked by the Inquisition. This book is evidence of Eckhart's careful study of the famous classic born in the twilight of the ancient Roman world, *De Consolatione Philosophiae,* The Consolations of Philosophy, by Boethius, loved by Alfred the Great, who translated it into Anglo-Saxon; by Chaucer, who was to translate it into English before 1382; by Queen Elizabeth, who rendered it in the English of her time, and by many others. Aside from its theological teachings, his *Book of Divine Comfort* shows Eckhart's appreciation of Boethius and other classical writers.

The constant travel necessitated by his administrative work brought Eckhart into contact with people and events in central, southern and western Germany, in France, and in Italy. As a result, it is natural that the heads of the Order felt that Meister Eckhart was the ideal man to assume the post of Superior of the entire Dominican Province in Germany. However, a certain conservatism within the Order itself, apparently based on fear of Eckhart's skill as an orator and disputant, his broad knowledge of places, and familiarity with the ways of men in all walks of life prevailed, and his nomination was never finalized.

In 1318, the year that Dante completed his *Divina Commedia,* Eckhart seems to have reached the summit of his development as a preacher. He was in Strassburg at this time, where he served as a preacher and prior. Two years later, in 1320, at the age of sixty, Eckhart received a most important honor: he was called by the Franciscan, Heinrich von Virneberg, Archbishop of Cologne, to assume a professorship in the college there. However, the brightness of this distinction was not long to remain undimmed. Already in the shadows the agents of the Inquisition waited, listening, watching, preparing for the day when this eloquent preacher of the Gospel, this scholar and author, so beloved by the common people who flocked to his sermons, would overstep the limits of prescribed dogma. And it was not long before they believed that they had evidence sufficient to convict him of heresy.

By 1325 several charges had been brought against Meister Eckhart in letters addressed to the Superiors of the Dominican Order at its headquarters in Venice. A few months later, the Archbishop of Cologne who already had had sufficient trouble with so-called "mystical societies" which had sprung up along the Rhine in areas under his jurisdiction, decided that heresy certainly could not be allowed to set foot within the precincts of the college itself. Therefore he agreed that the moment had arrived when charges against this too-popular preacher should be laid before the Inquisition. However, a Dominican managed to obtain the task of investigating Meister Eckhart, and naturally it did not take long for the former to report that he found his fellow-Dominican entirely without guilt or taint of heresy.

But the matter did not stop there. Perhaps sensing that if Franciscans had undertaken the examination things might have turned out differently, the Archbishop called in two experts in heresy, the Franciscans Benherus Friso and Peter de Estate. They were given the task to thoroughly examine Eckhart's writings and the reports of his sermons. It was not long before an extensive list of "errors" in doctrine had been assembled, and Eckhart in turn replied by means of his famous *Rechtfertigungsschrift,* Defense.

On January 24, 1327 Eckhart was required to answer the charges brought against him before the court of the Archbishop of Cologne. About three weeks later he preached in a Cologne church in defense of his ideas, and said that if there were any errors of faith in his writings or sermons, he would retract them gladly, for he certainly considered himself no heretic, and he appealed to Rome, as he was entitled to do under the rights of his Order. However, on February 22, Eckhart was informed that his application to Rome had been refused.

On March 27, 1329 Pope John XXII issued a bull describing certain of Meister Eckhart's teachings as contrary to church dogma. But Eckhart was no longer alive to know of his condemnation as one who had been led astray "by the father of lies, who often appears as an angel of light." This official fiat would doubtless have seriously shaken the soul of one whose life had been devoted to a defense and practise of the tenets from which that organized power had drawn its life-breath.

2.

When Meister Eckhart was forty years of age, Johannes Tauler was born in the city of Strassburg in the Papal Jubilee year of 1300, two years before the death of the painter, Cimabue. At the age of fifteen he entered the Dominican monastery where Eckhart was professor of theology. One can imagine the effect of the older Dominican teacher upon the impressionable mind of the young student, who well may have listened to those evening mealtime conversations Eckhart brought together in the little book mentioned above. Eventually Tauler entered the Dominican college in Cologne not long before Eckhart was named professor in that institution.

The year 1324 saw the climax of a struggle between Louis IV, king of Germany, and Pope John XXII, which had been increasing steadily for nearly a decade. Fearing that the German king's policy of personal ambition would lead to a weakening of the papal position in France as well as Germany, the Pope called upon the German ruler to abdicate, saying that no one could rightfully wear the German crown who did not have the Pope's express approval to do so. Louis angrily refused, with the result that the Pope declared him deposed and excommunicate. Therefore, in this year 1324, Strassburg, along with other cities and towns of Germany, was placed under a papal interdict.

But the times were against the Pope and his French ally, Charles IV, whom he hoped to see on the German throne. The German princes condemned in no uncertain terms the papal interference in German affairs, and the Electors sided with the princes. This attitude was also shared by many of the clergy in Germany, for despite the papal ban, church services continued in some places, and the sacraments were administered to the people.

Johannes Tauler was among those in Strassburg who refused to discontinue their priestly functions of celebrating the Mass and preaching to their congregations. With great courage, in defiance of both papal ban and agents of the Inquisition, he said, "While the Church can refuse us the sacrament externally, nobody can take away the spiritual joy of our oneness with God, and nobody can rob us of the privilege of taking the sacrament spiritually."

In 1339, the year before the birth of Geoffrey Chaucer in London, Tauler left Strassburg for a journey which was to have important results for his life work. On his travels he came into contact—particularly in Basel—with Swiss and German members of the famous group of mystics called the *Gottesfreunde,* The Friends of God.

The struggle for power between rival rulers in Germany, together with the interdict of the Pope, brought great hardship to the people. Some areas of the country were not freed from the papal ban for as much as twenty-six years, and the people were in great distress for lack of spiritual help and consolation.

Abnormal natural phenomena also began to appear, as though the forces of Nature had joined with spiritual and temporal rulers to make the lot of men as hard as possible. Torrential rains repeatedly destroyed the crops, just before harvest time. The rivers rose in devastating floods several years in succession, making spring planting difficult if not impossible. The winters were severely cold, so that men and animals suffered exceedingly. As a consequence, a series of famines swept the countryside, taking a dreadful toll of human life.

Convinced that they were living in the "last days" of the earth, men saw in all the events around them the fulfillment of prophecies of the Apocalypse of John. During these years southern Germany and Switzerland were visited by repeated earthquakes, one of which shook Basel with such force that the city was reduced to a heap of ruins. In the heavens appeared "signs and wonders" prophesied by the Scriptures: mysterious lights flashed upon the skies, men reported strange conditions of cloud and mist, and the stars seemed about to cast themselves upon the earth.

Visited by these dire external events, harassed by doubt and insecurity on every side, men withdrew more and more into themselves, seeking the sources of piety and devotion in their hearts. Lacking spiritual consolation from the church, suffering the desolation wrought by flood and famine, sword and fire, the people sought the essential truths of life in their personal experience. And in their search for the verities of existence, men reached out to one another in fraternal love and a spirit of true humanity.

Thus the Friends of God came into being. It was a free association of human beings in the sense that it was not a sect, had no dogma, no common form of religious devotion or practice, no common political outlook. The only desire the Friends of God shared in common was to strengthen one another in their living relationship with God and the spiritual world. They established "brotherhood houses" as retreat centers in certain areas where a number of the Friends of God were living.

One of the outstanding figures among the Friends of God was the wealthy banker of Strassburg, Rulman Merswin. His story is somewhat typical of that of many another layman who found himself drawn to the Friends of God. Born of a good family of Strassburg in 1307, Rulman Merswin was a man of business and high moral and ethical principles. By the time he was forty, due to his business acumen he had amassed a considerable fortune, and had married the daughter of one of the leading families of Strassburg. But although he had everything to give him pleasure, he was far from happy, and just after his fortieth birthday he decided that the time had come for him to take leave of the world, to devote himself and his wealth to the service of God, and to live as a celebate. His wife joined him on his mystical path. A few months later, on the day of Saint Martin, November 11, 1347, Merswin was walking in his garden in the evening, meditating on the way he and his wife had chosen, when suddenly he experienced a tremendous feeling of exaltation so that, as he later described it, it was as though he was whirled round and round his garden for sheer joy. But as quickly as the mood of exaltation came upon him, it left, and he slipped into a condition of despondency bordering upon despair. He began severe ascetic disciplines with the thought that these might relieve his inner struggle, but no light came.

At this time Johannes Tauler became his confessor, and Merswin told him of his suffering and his ascetic practices. Tauler at once forbade him to continue his self-imposed tortures, saying, "We are told to kill our passions, not our flesh and blood." Merswin obeyed, and only a short while later a Friend of God came to him and led him forward on the road to the spirit. He learned to depend quietly upon the guidance of the spirit alone, to subject himself to no code or rule of conduct, but to cultivate true humility, to seek anonymity, to cease self-assertion, to regard himself as a "captive of the Lord," to preserve the calmness of his soul like a stainless mirror, to attach less and less importance to himself in a worldly sense, and to think of himself only as "a hidden child of God."

On Octboer 9, 1364 Rulman Merswin had a dream in which he was told that a most important man would shortly visit him, and that in three years he would purchase land which would make a home of peace and rest for the Friends of God in Strassburg. Not long after this, Merswin was visited by a mysterious man whose name is most intimately connected with the whole story of the Friends of God. Called simply, "The Friend of God from the Oberland," he was long identified with the famous Nicholas of Basel, a noted Friend of God, who suffered martyrdom at the stake in Vienna for his convictions. Others have identified him with Rulman Merswin himself, as a sort of "double," while others believe that he never lived at all, but was a kind of ideal portrait of what the true Friend of God should be.

In any case, The Friend of God from the Oberland visited Merswin and told him that he had had a dream that Merswin would establish a retreat for the Friends of God at Strassburg. Merswin told him that he himself had had the same dream, and the Friend of God from the Oberland told him to wait quietly, to listen for the guidance of the Holy Spirit, and that at the end of three years he would know what was to be done.

In the Ill River near Strassburg was a little island called *daz Grüne Woerth,* The Green Island. In the twelfth century a convent had been established there, but had long since been deserted and had fallen into ruins. Early in October, 1367—just three years after his dream and his talk with the Friend of God from the Oberland—Merswin was walking by the river and saw the little island. Suddenly the realization flashed through him that this was the place he was to buy, that here he was to establish a house for the Friends of God. He promptly sought out the owner, paid him five hundred ten silver marks as the purchase price, and soon the convent building was repaired and a little chapel was constructed. Finally, on November 25, 1367 Merswin opened the house of the Friends of God on the Green Island, which became the center of a group of laymen who wished to live a purely mystical, religious life but without subjecting themselves to any external rule or official religious Order. Five years later Merswin completed arrangements whereby the group was acknowledged as a branch of the Knights of Saint John of Jerusalem, and the place became known as "The House of Saint John of the Green Island." Not long after this Merswin's wife died, and he spent his remaining years on the Green Island, devoting himself to the Friends of God who came there from far and near. Rulman Merswin died in the House of St. John of the Green Island on July 18, 1382. Four days after his death a sealed chest was opened which had been discovered in his room. Inside was a collection of manuscripts and letters, many of them in an unknown handwriting, giving details of instructions and advice by the Friend of God from the Oberland.

One of these manuscripts contained *The Story of the Master of Holy Scripture,* later included in a collection titled, *The Great Memorial.* According to the *Story of the Master of Holy Scripture,* the Friend of God from the Oberland one day arrived at a great city where a famous preacher was expounding the Bible to crowded and enthusiastic congregations. The Friend of God attended the sermons each day for five days. At the conclusion of the fifth day, he sought out the preacher and asked, "Reverend Sir, will you preach tomorrow on a theme I would suggest to you?" The clergyman agreed, and asked what the subject should be. The Friend of God from the Oberland replied, "How to attain the highest degree of spiritual life."

The preacher delivered a brilliant exposition the next morning. Starting from the Gospels he branched out into the Church Fathers, dipped deep into Dionysius, and concluded with a tremendous display of erudition. The congregation was enthralled by his words, but at the end of the service the theologian saw the Friend of God walk away silently and alone, with head bowed as though in deep thought.

The next day the Friend of God went to the clergyman and gave him a scathing criticism of the sermon, even saying that if that was the best he could do, then he was not capable of teaching about the spiritual life at all. The preacher's anger knew no bounds, but suddenly an inner voice told him to calm himself and to listen to the stranger's words. Having regained possession of himself once more, he quietly asked the Friend of God what help he could give him. Then the layman gave the Master of the Holy Scriptures twenty-three sentences, saying, "These are the ABC of religion; master these, and events will show their worth." The theologian withdrew from active service and spent a long time in meditation and prayer. His power of preaching left him, so that he could hardly speak an intelligible sentence, let alone deliver a whole sermon. His congregations deserted him; everywhere he was scorned and ridiculed.

After two years he was led by an inner voice which told him to enter the pulpit to preach during the service. Quietly he did so, noting the scorn and derision on the faces of the people as he faced them. For a long moment there was silence, then suddenly without any premeditation at all he gave out as his text, "Behold the Bridegroom cometh; go ye out to meet him!" And the spiritual power which flowed with his words was so great that it is said that forty persons fainted from sheer excitement and joy.

Tradition has long connected the "Master of Holy Scripture" with Johannes Tauler, and indicates that this is the account of his meeting with the Friend of God from the Oberland. Tauler became intimately acquainted with leading Friends of God in many places on his travels, and was deeply impressed with their way of life. As he said in a sermon at about this time, "The theologians of Paris study great tomes and turn over many pages, but the Friends of God read the living Book where everything is life."

Among the Friends of God whom Tauler met were Henry of Nördlingen, one of the outstanding representatives of the mysticism of the time, Hermann of Fritzlar, and two pious nuns, Christina Ebner, prioress of the Engelthal Convent near Nuremberg, and Margaretha Ebner, of the Convent of Maria Medingen in Swabia. One of the letters from the famous correspondence between Henry of Nördlingen and Margaretha Ebner is dated 1348, and asks that she "Pray for Tauler, who lives as a matter of course in the midst of great trial and testing because he teaches the truth and lives in conformity with it as perfectly as a preacher can."

Having visited Friends of God in many places during his seven years' absence from Strassburg, Tauler was convinced that a layman has tasks to perform which basically are as spiritually important as those of the clergy. In one of his sermons Tauler reflects the religious-social spirit he had found in the way of life of the Friends of God: "One can spin, another can make shoes, and all these are gifts of the Holy Ghost. I tell you, if I were not a priest, I would esteem it a great gift that I was able to make shoes, and I would try to make them so well that they would be a model to all."

One of the documents which has come down to us from the Friends of God is a public announcement which probably originated in Strassburg, and may have been written by Rulman Merswin himself. It was copied and recopied, and was circulated very widely in southern and western Germany during Tauler's lifetime. It is of interest because it gives a picture of the kind of appeal which was made to the public by the Friends of God in the latters' search for others who might be minded to join them:

"All those in whom the love of God or the terror brought about by the dreadful calamities of the present wakens a wish to begin a new and spiritual life, will discover great advantage in withdrawing into themselves every morning when they waken, in order to consider what they will do during the day. Should they find any evil thought in themselves, any purpose which is contrary to the divine will, let them give it up and cast it aside, to the glory of God. In the evening, upon going to bed, let them consider how they have spent the day. Let them recall what deeds they have done, and in what spirit they have performed them. If they discover that they have done any good, let them thank God, and give Him the glory. If they discover they have done evil, let them take the blame for it themselves, and lay the fault on nobody else, and let them deeply repent before God, saying to Him, 'O Lord, be merciful to me, and forgive all my sins of this day, for I sincerely repent, and I firmly intend from now on with Thy help, to avoid sinning.'"

In 1348 Strassburg was visited by the Black Death. All who could leave the city fled before the dread disease, and soon few except the sick were left behind. Even relatives, nurses and physicians left for fear of the pestilence. But among those who stayed in the city to care for the sick, to comfort the dying, and to bury the dead, was Johannes Tauler.

Week after week, month after month, this fearless Dominican stood in his pulpit in defiance of papal ban and the Black Death and bore witness to the truth that was in him. In one of his sermons He pointed out that "In all the world God desires and requires but one thing: that He find the noble ground he has laid in the noble soul of man bare and ready, so that He may do His noble divine work therein." Hence it is necessary that men "let God prepare their ground, and give themselves wholly to God and put away the self in all things."

But Tauler had no illusions about the trials that await man on his path of purification, on his way to the spirit: "When our heavenly Father determines to grace a particular soul with spiritual gifts, and to transform it in a special way, He does not purge it gently. Instead, He plunges it into a sea of bitterness, and deals with it as He did with the prophet Jonah."

He knew that "No teacher can teach what he has not

lived through himself," and he continued his work at Strassburg against all odds, encouraging others by his Christianity in action. He had said, "Never trust a virtue which has not been put into practice." Now he was practicing the virtue of a Friend of God, the virtue of devotion to his fellow-men. It is no wonder that Luther was to write of him, "Never in either the Latin or German language have I found more wholesome, purer teaching, nor any that more fully agrees with the Gospel." Tauler's words were tried and purified in the fire of personal experience.

It is related that the Friend of God from the Oberland gave Tauler two prayers which he was to use every morning and evening. They are significant examples of the spirit which animated the mystical striving of the Friends of God. "In the morning you are to say, 'O Lord, I wish to keep from all sin today. Help me to do everything I do today according to Thy divine will and to *Thy* glory, whether my *nature* likes it or not.' In similar fashion every evening you are to say, 'O Lord, I am a poor, unworthy creature. Be merciful to me, forgive my sins, for I repent of them and sincerely desire Thy help that I may commit no more.' "

Tauler's writings have great appeal even today because of their freshness, their closeness to everyday life, their common sense. They are not primarily Scholastic speculations like much of Eckhart's writing, but are nearer to the vigorous directness of the Reformers. Although Tauler loved, as he described it, "to put out into the deep and let down the nets" into the world of study and meditation, at the same time he cautioned that such "spiritual enjoyments are food of the soul, and are only to be taken for nourishment and support to help us in our active work." This thought was echoed in the spirit of the Reformation.

In the years following the Black Death and the papal ban, Tauler continued to make Strassburg the center of his work. He kept up his correspondence with many of the Friends of God, especially with Margaretha Ebner. His services were crowded, and his sermons were held in the highest regard by his congregations.

On the fifteenth of June, 1361 in the Convent of Saint Nikolaus in Strassburg, Johannes Tauler died at the age of sixty-one. Tradition relates that for him the moment of death was an experience of pure joy, for as he said in one of his last sermons, "Eternity is the everlasting Now."

3.

Linked with the name of Johannes Tauler as a Friend of God and a continuer of the work of Meister Eckhart is that of yet another Dominican, Heinrich Suso. Suso was born in 1295, five years before the birth of Tauler, in the town of Ueberlingen on the Lake of Constance. When he was still a small boy his parents decided he should study for the Church, and his preparatory education began at Constance, and was continued at Cologne, where he came under the influence of the teaching of Meister Eckhart.

Suso has revealed himself in his autobiography as a deeply emotional man, with a very unusual gift of expression. In his "glowing, vivid language," as it has been described, Suso pictures his mystical experiences in great detail, in contrast to the silence in which many other mystics have shrouded their strivings.

At about the age of eighteen, in 1313, the year Boccaccio was born in Florence, Suso entered a monastery in Constance. There he voluntarily subjected himself to the most severe ascetic ordeals. He centered his affection in an ideal which he personified under the name of the Eternal Wisdom. He relates how this figure appeared before him and said, "My son, give me your heart." He took a knife and cut deep into his chest the letters of the name Jesus, so that the scar-traces of each of the letters remained all his life, "about the length of a finger-joint," as he says.

Suso once saw a vision of angels, and asked them in what manner God dwelt in his soul. The angel told him to look within. He did so, and as he gazed he saw that "his body over his heart was as clear as crystal, and in the center sat tranquilly, the lovely form of the Eternal Wisdom. Beside her sat, filled with heavenly longing, the servitor's own soul, which, leaning lovingly toward God's side, and encircled by His arms, lay pressed close to His heart." Suso wrote his autobiography in the third person, and referred to himself as "the servitor of the Divine Wisdom," much as Swedenborg in a later century was to refer to himself in his writings as "the servant of the Lord Jesus Christ."

Heinrich Suso took the expression, "No cross, no crown," with terrible literalness. He imposed fearful penances upon himself, and consumed sixteen long years in cruel austerity. For example, he relates how he donned a hair shirt, and bound himself with a heavy iron chain, but at length he had to give these up, since the loss of blood they occasioned was too much for his strength to bear. Instead he fashioned a crude night-shirt which he wore next to his skin. In this garment he sewed a series of leather straps in which sharp tacks were fitted to that they pierced his skin with his slightest movement. Later he made a cross of wood as tall as himself, and the cross-beam the length of his outstretched arms. Into this he drove thirty nails, and wore the cross fastened to his bare back, the nails pointing into his flesh. He bore this instrument of torture for some eight years, day and night. Finally, after sixteen years of agony, Suso had a vision at Whitsuntide in which he was assured that God no longer wished him to continue his austerities. Only then did he abate the severity of his asceticism, and threw his instruments of self-torture into a running stream near the monastery.

In his autobiography Suso relates that one time he prayed that God would instruct him how to suffer. In response, he had a vision of Christ on the cross in the likeness of a seraphic being with six wings. On each pair of wings the legend was inscribed, "Receive suffering willingly; Bear suffering patiently; Learn suffering in the way of Christ."

The result of this almost unbelievable "receiving, bearing, learning" of suffering was a man whose gentleness and calm, lyric beauty of speech won hearts to his teaching. The fires of affliction had nearly consumed him to ashes, yet, phoenix-like, his spirit rose anew in a sweetness of expression and a grandeur of soul which one could scarcely resist. In 1335, the year Giotto began his work on the Cathedral at Florence, Suso set out on his wanderings through Swabia as a traveling preacher. He advanced the spiritual teachings of Eckhart, but through his mystical fervor they were permeated by a newness, a spontaneous grace and a transcendent beauty. And something of this spirit which was reborn in Suso comes down to us today in his autobiography, issued in 1365, which has established itself as a unique work of its kind, and as "one of the most interesting and charming of all autobiographies." Suso's preaching was especially popular among the nuns of the convents he visited. Their hearts were deeply impressed by the obvious, overwhelming sincerity and fervor of his manner and words.

Heinrich Suso's writings are among the classics of mysticism. His first work, *Das Büchlein der Wahrheit,* The Little Book of Truth, was written in Cologne in 1329, and springs directly from the mystical teachings of Meister Eckhart. Somewhat later, in Constance he wrote of the more practical aspects of mysticism in his *Das Büchlein der Ewigen Weisheit,* The Little Book of Eternal Wisdom. This book has been called "the finest fruit of German mysticism."

Something of the romanticism of the troubadour of the Ages of Faith, the charm of days gone by, the sad evanescence of the dream of chivalry and the heroic ideals of knighthood lives in the mystical expressions of Suso. He develops a mood of gentleness, of tender, delicate imagery which sets him apart from all the other men whose lives we are considering here.

Concerning his books, Suso wrote, "Whoever will read these writings of mine in a right spirit can hardly fail to be stirred in his heart's depths, either to fervent love, or to new light, or to longing and thirsting for God, or to detestation and loathing of his sins, or to that spiritual aspiration by which the soul is renewed in grace." These words gain "fearful symmetry," to use Blake's phrase, when we recall that they were written by one who, for example, had practised such abstinence in eating and drinking, that often as he stood with his brother monks in choir at Compline, when the holy water was sprinkled over the group during the service, he opened his parched mouth toward the aspergillum in the hope that even a single drop of water might cool his burning thirst. Such a man can write about "longing and thirsting" as very few who have walked this earth have been able to do.

About 1348, his wandering in central and southern Germany having come to an end, this love-inspired Swabian poet-knight of the spirit, singer of the glories of Eternal Wisdom, settled at last in Ulm on the river Donau. There he died on the Day of Damascus, the anniversary of St. Paul's first mystical vision of the Risen Christ, January 25, 1366, at the age of seventy-one.

Through the Dominican stream the Scholasticism of Thomas Aquinas came to Meister Eckhart in the form of ideas which he shaped and fashioned into aphoristic expression by means of his remarkable powers of thinking; in the hands of Johannes Tauler Scholasticism was transformed into Christian action, into practical deeds of will; in the golden warmth of his loving, devoted heart Heinrich Suso bathed Scholasticism in a lyric splendor of poetic imagery so that it became a thing of transcendent, eternal beauty.

4.

Jan van Ruysbroeck was born in the little village of Ruysbroeck on the Senne between Brussels and Hal in 1293, the year after the death of the English Franciscan philosopher and scientist, Roger Bacon. When Jan was eleven years old he decided to run away from home in order that he might more completely dedicate himself and his life to God. He went to the house of his uncle, Jan Hinckaert in Brussels, and asked if the latter would undertake to educate him to the service of God. The uncle, who was a Canon of the Church of Saint Gudale in Brussels, arranged that the boy would live in his home and study with his friend, the learned priest, Franc van Coudenberg, and himself. Eventually Jan took the four year course in the Latin School of Brussels, and from there he attended the well-known theological school in Cologne.

At the age of twenty-four Jan van Ruysbroeck was ordained a priest, and was appointed chaplain to his uncle in Brussels. His life for the next two decades seems to have been that of a dedicated pastor, who served his congregation to the best of his ability, but was not otherwise particularly distinguished, at least externally.

However, as Jan van Ruysbroeck's fiftieth birthday approached, he had a remarkable experience. He felt that the time had come when he was to withdraw from active work in the world, and that he was called to devote himself entirely to spiritual matters. At about the same time his uncle was deeply confused and depressed one day, and an inner voice directed him to go into the church. As he did so, he saw that a visiting missionary priest had just mounted the pulpit to preach to the congregation. Now the uncle knew that this priest had a serious speech defect. To the uncle's astonishment, as the missionary opened his mouth, the words flowed out in a river of eloquence! At this, the preacher turned to where the uncle was standing and said, "This miracle has happened for the sake of that man standing there, in order that he will repent and turn to God."

In similar manner, van Coudenberg also had a spiritual experience, and was filled with the deep desire to live a more dedicated life.

At Easter, 1343 the three men resigned their work in Brussels and went deep into the forest of Soignes where they found a deserted hunting-lodge called *Grönendal*, The Green Valley. The place had not been used for over a generation, and the men set to work to make a home for themselves there, and soon had built a chapel. Others joined them, and before long a small community had developed.

After about six years the community decided to take on the rule and habit of the Augustinian canons. And the moving spirit was Jan van Ruysbroeck himself, who was as devoted to practical tasks as he was to spiritual matters. Whether it was necessary to repair a stove, load a manure cart, discuss deep problems of theology, or nurse the sick, he was always ready and cheerfully willing to do whatever was to be done.

The fame of the little forest community spread, and visitors came from far places to see the life that was being lived there. One day two young priests, theological students from the University of Paris, arrived and asked to speak with Jan van Ruysbroeck. They wished his advice concerning their spiritual development, and begged that he would help them to find the way to the spirit, and would speak with them about the condition of their souls. His reply was to the point: "You are as spiritual as you have the desire to be, that is all." They were somewhat annoyed at the abruptness of his words, and turned away. At once he spoke to them in a loving tone: "My very dear children, I said your spirituality was what you wish it to be so that you would understand that your spirituality is entirely in proportion to your good will. Then enter into yourselves; don't ask others about your progress. Examine your good will, and from that alone you will discover the measure of your spirituality."

One of the guests at Grönendal was Johannes Tauler, who was much impressed with the life he saw there. In turn, Tauler doubtless told Jan van Ruysbroeck about his experiences with the Friends of God.

In 1378, the year after Gregory XI condemned John Wycliffe, translator of the Vulgate into English, as a heretic, the famous lay-preacher, Gerard Groote visited the community of Grönendal and had many conversations with Jan van Ruysbroeck.

Gerard Groote was born in the town of Deventer, about sixty miles from Amsterdam in 1340. His parents were wealthy, and at the age of fifteen Gerard was sent to the University of Paris. In three years he was given his Master's degree, and then was called to teach at Cologne, where he was soon advanced to the position of professor of philosophy, and also received important appointments of a civil nature.

One day Groote was standing with a crowd watching a game in a Cologne square when a modestly dressed stranger, with a serious, sincere face approached him and spoke to him softly: "Why are you standing here? You ought to become *another man*." Soon after this incident Groote fell seriously ill, and his life was despaired of. However, when matters were at their worst, he recalled the words of the stranger, and at once promised Heaven that he would do everything in his power to become "another man" if he was allowed to regain his health. Groote recovered, and not long after was sought out by his former teacher from the University of Paris, Henry de Kalkar, who for some years had been the prior of a Carthusian monastery near Deventer. This dedicated man had come to Groote, impelled by an inner urge to call the latter to a new life.

Groote retired from the world, and dedicated himself to the pursuit of spiritual things. Eventually the time came when his studies entitled him to be ordained a priest. This he refused, and refused repeatedly to the end of his life.

In 1379 Groote sensed a spiritual call to go out into the

countryside as an itinerant lay-preacher. The Bishop of Utrecht granted him a license as a preacher, allowing him to speak anywhere in his diocese.

According to all accounts Groote was a speaker of marked excellence. He differed radically from other preachers of his time in that he never threatened his hearers with punishments of hell nor sought to bribe them with the bliss of heaven. He spoke simply and directly to them of the love of God, the great way of salvation, the search for the good, and always about the wonderful possibilities of a life lived in consonance with God. He spoke only from his personal experience, never used any Latin phrases in his discourses, and employed only the simplest, most direct forms of expression. The result was that for five years people flocked to hear him wherever he went.

In the course of his wanderings Groote visited Grönendal, and was deeply impressed by everything he saw, and most of all by the entirely practical attitude toward life which Jan van Ruysbroeck manifested. The result was that Groote was inspired to form a community, a kind of Christian brotherhood, which would be bound by no permanent vows as were monks, but would consist of individuals who freely chose to live together in poverty, chastity, obedience, simplicity and piety, holding all possessions in common as the early Christians had done, and working together to earn their own livelihood.

Groote was soon surrounded by a group of men who enthusiastically wished to take up this life, and who took the name, "The Brotherhood of the Common Lot" or "the Common Life." The first community house was established at Deventer, and was called a "brother house." Soon "sister houses" for women were also established. Groote loved books, and therefore he freely gave his fortune for the purchase of rare books which the brothers and sisters copied by hand—this of course was before the invention of the printing press—and the money received from the sale of these volumes was used for the maintenance of the communities. The Brothers and Sisters of the Common Life mingled freely with the world, and soon came to be recognized everywhere in Holland, Belgium and in the German Rhine valley by their plain grey habit and their simple, unassuming manners. Their life was devoted to the care of orphan children, the spreading of knowledge through the sale of books that they copied, and in the teaching of reading and writing to adults. Their method of instruction of children was based on practical life, and was directed toward moral and spiritual improvement. They taught the children under their care to earn a living, but never encouraged them to enter a profession which would give them undue wealth.

Jan van Ruysbroeck's last days were spent quietly in the community at Grönendal, and many stories were told of his remarkable spiritual development. For example he was missing one day, and at last was found sitting beneath a tree in the forest, sunk in deep meditation, while according to the tale, the tree itself was surrounded by a heavenly brightness of shimmering colors.

He knew the force of directness in conversation. A man once tried to draw him out on the subject of the dreadful wickedness in the world. His only remark was, "What we are, that we behold; and what we behold, that we are."

Like all mystics, he loved animals and flowers, and his greatest earthly joy was in the song of the birds of the forest. His death took place in 1381, the year of the outbreak of the Peasant Revolt in England under the leadership of Wat Tyler, and the priest, John Ball. Stories tell how at the moment of his death, the bells of the churches in neighboring villages began to toll all by themselves, and how after several years when his corpse was exhumed it showed no decomposition, but gave off a sweet odor which healed the sick who were brought near.

Gerhart Groote survived Jan van Ruysbroeck by three years. Meanwhile, a young man had joined the circle of the Brotherhood of the Common Life who is known as the author of one of the most important books of devotion in the world. His name was Thomas à Kempis, and his *Imitatio Christi,* Imitation of Christ, is a classic which has inspired men throughout the centuries since it first appeared. Thomas also was the biographer of Gerhard Groote, and his impression of the Brotherhood of the Common Life was, "I never before recall having seen men so devout, so full of love for God and their fellow-men. Living in the world, they were altogether unworldly."

At the conclusion of Thomas' Life of Gerhard Groote is a collection of aphorisms which he attributes to the latter as among the basic teachings of the Brotherhood of the

Common Life: "Conquer yourself. Turn your heart from things, and direct your mind continually to God. Do not for any cause allow yourself to lose your composure. Practice obedience, and accept things that are difficult. Continually exercise yourself in humility and moderation. The further one knows himself to be from perfection, the closer he is to it. Of all temptations, the greatest is not to be tempted at all. Never breathe so much as a word to display your religion or learning. Nothing is a better test of a man than to hear himself praised. Above all, and first of all, let Christ be the basis of your study and the mirror of your life."

Years after the deaths of Jan van Ruysbroeck and Gerhard Groote, a twelve-year old boy was brought to the Brethren of the Common Life at Deventer, and was placed in the school there. Destined to be one of the most important figures of the Reformation period, Desiderius Erasmus, became famous for his modesty, his temperance and wisdom. These qualities are no doubt traceable to the early training he received at the hands of the Brethren of the Common Life. Erasmus of Rotterdam advised moderation and tolerance, even when the opposite qualities ran high, as for example in his famous letter in reply to the Pope's invitation to come to Rome in order to advise him on how to deal with Luther and his followers: "You ask me what you should do. Some believe there is no remedy but force. I do not believe this, for I think there would be dreadful bloodshed. . . . If you intend to try prison, lash, stake and scaffold, you do not need my help. . . .

Discover the roots of the disease and clean them out first of all. Punish nobody, but let what has happened be considered as a visitation of Providence, and extend a general amnesty to all." Had the moderation counselled in this letter, typical of the spirit of the Brotherhood of the Common Life, been followed, how different might the course of history have been!

5.

In 1401, when Ghiberti's Baptistry doors, "worthy to be the gates of Paradise," were first shown to the admiring eyes of his fellow Florentines, and the English Parliament decreed that all proven heretics were to be burned at the stake, Nicolas Chrypffs was born at Cusa on the Moselle River. Nicolas was to be known as "the last great philosopher of the dying Middle Ages," and was to fling wide the doors of men's minds to the concept of a universe which is infinite. As a student he made a brilliant record in his study of law and mathematics at the renowned University of Padua, and followed this with a course in theology at Cologne where, as we have seen, he was preceded by Meister Eckhart, Tauler, Suso, van Ruysbroeck, and Groote. Eventually Nicolas became Archdeacon of Liège at about the time that Joan of Arc was burned at the stake in Rouen.

The Council of Basel, which had convened intermittently since 1417, was beginning its last ten years of existence when Nicolas attended its sessions in his official capacity as Archdeacon of Liège, in 1437. These sessions took place at the time when Cosimo de Medici was making preparations for the opening of his famous Platonic Academy in Florence, the institution renowned as a center of the revival of the learning of the classical world.

Shortly after his attendance at the Council of Basel, Nicolas was sent to Constantinople to try his efforts toward the solution of one of the most vexing problems of the time, the reunion of the churches of East and West. His work at Basel and Constantinople attracted the attention of the Pope, so that in 1440 Nicolas was sent to Germany as papal legate at a very critical moment in the relations between Germany and the Church of Rome.

When Nicolas arrived in Germany, Frederick, Duke of Styria was chosen king to rule as Frederick IV. Just at that time the Council of Basel had appointed an "anti-pope,' called Felix V, in opposition to Pope Eugenius IV. In the fact that soon after his election, Frederick decided to extend his influence to the support of Eugenius in opposition to the Council of Basel, one perhaps can see the fruit of the work of Nicolas of Cusa as papal legate in Germany.

It also seems something more than coincidence that in 1448, when Frederick IV and Pope Nicolas V signed the Concordat of Vienna, by which the German church was firmly rebound to Rome, Nicolas of Cusa was raised to the rank of Cardinal. Two years later he was appointed Bishop of Britten.

The reactionary character of the Concordat of Vienna made impossible any reform of conditions within the German church. The clergy in Germany who had hoped for some easing of the repressive measures of the papacy, were doomed to disappointment. On the other hand, the Concordat of Vienna was one of the principal links in the chain of events that finally culminated on All Saints' Day, 1517, when Martin Luther nailed his theses to the door of the church in Wittenberg, and the German Reformation became a fact.

The sixteen years (1448-1464) of the Cardinalate of Nicolas of Cusa coincide with remarkable developments in the social and cultural life of the Western world. The year 1452 is notable as the year of the birth of two men of marked divergence of outlook. The first was Girolamo Savonarola, the Dominican monk, leader of the reaction against the Renaissance, the dogmatic eschatologist from Ferrara, who as "dictator of Florence" held a brief sway over the minds and bodies of men of his time. Also in 1452 was born the genius of the Renaissance, the archetype of the "new man," the very incarnation of the spirit of progress, of universality, of investigation, of freedom from traditionalism and conservatism—Leonardo da Vinci. At this same time a host of the world's most famous Greek scholars left Constantinople in fear of the advancing Turks under Mohammed II, who finally took the city the following year, which also marked the end of the Hundred Years' War in Western Europe.

In 1454, as a kind of picture of things to come in the field of technical development and invention, Johannes Gutenberg issued his first texts printed with movable type, and before two more years were completed, published his edition of the Vulgate Bible at Mainz. 1456 is notable as the year the Turks captured Athens and subsequently all Greece, thus marking the end of the last vestiges of classicism remaining in that country.

Pico della Mirandola, famous Renaissance scholar and writer, collector of precious books and manuscripts, master of Greek, Latin, Hebrew, Chaldee and Arabic, student of the mysticism of the Kabbalah and other mystical writings, was born in 1463. The following year, on the 11th of August, Nicolas of Cusa died, renowned as a distinguished prince of the Church, and as a diplomat traveling in the service of the Pope.

Today Nicolas of Cusa is remembered for his cosmological conceptions, his originality and breadth of thought, and his courage as a thinker at a time when the rationalized dogmatic system of Scholasticism was breaking down in face of the impact of the new age. As the famous French mathematician and philosopher, René Descartes was to write nearly two hundred years after Nicolas' death, "The Cardinal of Cusa and several other theologians have supposed the world to be infinite, and the Church has never condemned them for it. On the contrary, it is thought that to make His works appear very great is one way to honor God." Nicolas of Cusa's work was appreciated by such men as Giordano Bruno, philosopher, poet, and martyr, Johannes Kepler, the astronomer, and Descartes, to name but a few. The courage necessary for a thinker to grasp the implications of the new age was present in Nicolas of Cusa, and the scope of his investigations in the world of thought is evidence of his importance and stature.

6.

The year 1487 is regarded by some as the year of the beginning of the Renaissance. By others it is remembered as the time the Portuguese navigator, Bartholomeu Diaz, sailing along the African coast on a voyage of exploration, discovered the Cape of Good Hope and thereby opened the passage to India and China. Still others recall that this was the year of the birth of one Henry Cornelius, generally known as Agrippa of Nettesheim, in the city of Cologne on September 14, 1487. His family was honored for its service to the royal house of Hapsburg, but little is known of his childhood and youth.

Like others whom we have considered, Henry Cornelius studied at the University of Cologne. He also learned eight languages, and passed some time in France while still a young man.

In 1486, the year before Henry Cornelius was born, the son of Frederick IV, whom Nicolas of Cusa had supported in signing the Concordat of Vienna, came to the throne of Germany as Maximilian I. The latter was heir to great areas of Austria, was administrator of the Netherlands, and not long after he came to the throne of Germany he united the country, and through the marriage of his son Philip to the heiress of the Spanish kingdoms, his influence soon spread to that country as well. Thus Maximilian exercised a power in Europe as had no German ruler for centuries.

While he was still a young man, Henry Cornelius was appointed secretary in the service of Maximilian, and his life of travel and adventure began almost at once. However, the life of the battlefield and the court did not suit him, and not long afterward we find him at the University of Dôle as a lecturer on philosophy. This appointment was made in 1509, the year that Erasmus wrote his *Chiliades adagiorum,* by which his reputation as an author was established.

But Henry Cornelius' lectures did not long escape the attention of the Inquisition, and he went to England on a diplomatic mission for Maximilian as the result of an attack made upon him by the monk, John Catilinet who was lecturing at Ghent. In London Henry Cornelius was a welcome guest in the home of Dr. John Colet, friend and later the patron of Erasmus, student of the teachings of Savonarola, former lecturer at Oxford, at that time dean of St. Paul's Cathedral. In his later life, Colet was to preach on the occasion of Wolsey's installation as Cardinal, and was to become chaplain to Henry VIII. He did much to introduce the humanist teachings of the Renaissance into England, and was an outspoken opponent of auricular confession and the celibacy of the clergy of the Catholic Church.

After his return to the Continent, Henry Cornelius went to Italy with Maximilian on one of the latter's expeditions against Venice. During his stay in Italy in 1512, the year the Medici were recalled to Florence, and Martin Luther was made a Doctor of Theology, he attended the Council of Pisa as a theologian. This council had been called by a group of Cardinals in opposition to militaristic plans of Pope Julius II who had laid the cornerstone for the new basilica of St. Peter's in Rome six years before.

In all, Henry Cornelius remained in Italy about seven years, and they were a very eventful time, for they coincided with some of the most important events of the Renaissance period. In these years the Aldine edition of Plato appeared in Venice, Niccolo Machiavelli wrote *The Prince,* a landmark in the history of political thought, and Erasmus published his New Testament in Greek. Julius II died during this period, and Giovanni de Medici, made Cardinal at fourteen, now became Pope Leo X, whose famous exclamation, "Since God has given us the papacy, let us enjoy it," set a pattern for the Renaissance, while his permission to sell indulgences for the benefit of the construction of St. Peter's led to the upheaval of the Reformation.

Henry Cornelius was active as a physician during his first years in Italy, first in the household of the Marquis of Monferrato, later in that of the Duke of Savoy. In 1515 he accepted an invitation to lecture at the University of Pavia on one of the works of the ancient world beloved by the adherents of the new learning of the Renaissance, the *Pimander* of Hermes Trismegistus. This was the year when Sir Thomas More wrote his *Utopia,* and Leonardo da Vinci left Rome for the last time enroute to his three-year exile and death in France.

The university lectures on the *Pimander* were suddenly broken off as a result of the victorious advance into Italy by the armies of Francis I of France. Henry Cornelius returned to Germany, and in 1518, the year Zwingli began the Reformation among the Swiss, he was appointed town advocate of Metz. But he was not left in peace for long. First, the death of Maximilian at the beginning of 1519 and the subsequent election of Charles V, King of Spain, Naples, Sicily, ruler of the Netherlands, Austria, Burgundy, and of dominions in the New World, to be ruler of Germany brought changes in the life of Henry Cornelius. Second, a woman was tried in Metz for witchcraft. In his position as town advocate Henry Cornelius went to her defense, with the result that he became involved in a serious controversy with one of the most dreaded agents of the Inquisition, the notorious Nicholas Savin. Finally, in 1520, the year of Magellan's voyage around the world, of the death of the painter, Raphael, and of Luther's burning of the papal bull, Henry Cornelius quietly left Metz for Cologne, where he remained in discreet retirement for about two years.

He appeared in public life once more, first in Geneva, afterward in Freiburg, where he practiced as a physician. In 1524, a year before Tyndale's English translation of the New Testament appeared, he went to Lyons to accept a post as physician to Louise of Savoy, mother of Francis I. But the unsettled times—now accentuated by the terrible sack of Rome by the armies of Constable Bourbon in 1527 —caused him to relinquish the position in favor of some post further north which might offer greater security for his study and work.

That Henry Cornelius was considered an able scholar is evidenced by the fact that at about this time he was offered the opportunity to participate in a disputation concerning the legality of the divorce action between Henry VIII of England and Catharine of Aragon, which was then taking place. However, he accepted an offer to be archivist and historian to Charles V, which Louise of Savoy obtained for him.

The death of Louise of Savoy in 1531 weakened his position, and in addition to all of the other ferment of the time, the news that Henry VIII had declared himself "Supreme Head of the Church of England" only increased the uncertainty of conditions. Henry Cornelius also had published several works which had attracted the attention of the Inquisition, and for a time he was imprisoned in Brussels. However, despite the publication of his *De occulta philosophia,* Concerning Secret Science, written about 1510, printed in Antwerp 1531, which the Inquisition did their best to prevent, Henry Cornelius was able to live for some time at Cologne and Bonn under the personal protection of the great Hermann von Wied, Archbishop of Cologne, who recognized and appreciated his remarkable qualities as a scholar and man.

At the very end of his life, while he was visiting Paris, Francis I had him arrested on the strength of a report that he had spoken badly of the reputation of the queen mother. The charge was proven false and he was released after a brief imprisonment, but the strain of the experience was too great for him to bear, and he died suddenly at Grenoble on February 18, 1535 at the age of forty-nine. His death took place in the same year as that of Sir Thomas More, and five years after that of Erasmus.

Henry Cornelius was married three times, and was the father of a large family of children. His memory—despite attacks on his reputation and teachings by the Inquisition long after his death—has been kept alive through the years because of his writings, mainly his *De occulta philosophia.* A man of unusual courage and in some ways a kind of universal genius, Henry Cornelius was typical of the men whose lives spanned the period that opened the way to the modern age.

7.

Columbus had reached America on his western voyage; Lorenzo de Medici had died in Florence; the Spaniard, Rodrigo Borgia, along with his mistress and children now inhabited the Vatican as Pope Alexander VI, whose frankly pagan orgies were more fitting to the later Roman emperors than to the Vicar of Christ upon earth; and in the little Swiss town of Einsiedeln in Canton Schwyz, the local physician, illegitimate son of a Grand Master of the Teutonic Order, was in turn the father of a son whom he named Theophrastus Bombast von Hohenheim. Later the son himself chose the name by which he is known to history—Paracelsus.

The boy's early education was in the hands of his father;

at the age of sixteen he entered the University of Basel. However, his restless nature and his independent thinking made formal study most unattractive to him, and he determined to seek an education in his own way.

About this time he heard of the great Benedictine scholar, Johannes Trithemius, originally Abbot of the Monastery of Würzburg, later of Sponheim near Kreuznach. The Abbot of Sponheim was celebrated for the remarkable library he had collected, for his studies in cryptography, for his writings on history, and for his researches in alchemy and related sciences. This same Abbot of Sponheim had greatly influenced Henry Cornelius in the latter's work on his *De occulta philosophia*.

Paracelsus decided to apply to the Abbot of Sponheim for the opportunity to study science with him. He was accepted, but the association did not last very long. Led by a desire to learn more about the nature and properties of minerals first-hand, he went to the Tyrolean mines owned by the famous merchant-administrators and bankers to the German Emperors, the Fuggers.

Paracelsus felt at home among the miners. He soon came to the conviction that what he gained through direct observation was the best education of all. He learned about the processes involved in mining operations, the nature of ores, the properties of mineral waters, and the stratification of the rocks of the earth. Meanwhile he came to know the home life of the miners, studied their illnesses and the types of accidents to which they were most prone. In brief, from his experiences in the mines he concluded that formal schooling is not education in the mysteries of nature. He was convinced that only by reading the book of nature first-hand and through personal contact with those who work with nature can one come to anything like truly natural scientific knowledge.

This point of view followed Paracelsus throughout his life, and colored his relationships with those scholars with whom he came into contact. He based his work entirely on the results of his own observation and experience, and not on theories acquired from others.

Paracelsus wandered over a great part of central Europe in order that he might come to a direct personal knowledge of things. He once said that the physician must read the book of nature, and that to do so he must "walk over its pages." He came to the conclusion that since the temperaments, constitutions and activities of different peoples are different, the diseases from which they suffer must also be different. Therefore he believed that it was incumbent upon the physician to know other peoples as the key to understanding his own.

The summation of Paracelsus' method of study is contained in his questions, "From where do I obtain all my secrets, from what authors? It would be better if one asked how the animals have learned their skills. If nature can teach irrational animals, can it not much more teach men?"

In all, Paracelsus spent nearly a full decade in his wanderings in search of knowledge. At the end of his travels, while the mass of information he had gathered lacked order and coherence, there is no doubt that here was a man whose experiences, observations of peoples, places and events, as well as knowledge of the elements and processes of nature gave his words and deeds the weight of direct evidence. His superiority to his contemporaries was unquestionable.

When Paracelsus returned to Basel in 1527 he was appointed city physician, and also was made professor of physic, medicine, and surgery at the University. He undertook to give a course of lectures in medicine, but the latter provoked a storm of protest because they were so unconventional, as might have been expected from one holding his views on education. First of all, Paracelsus lectured in German, not Latin, which was unheard of in academic circles of the time. Then his lectures were composed of statements derived from his experience, and presented his own methods of cure, based upon his personal points of view. But worst of all to the traditionalists, Paracelsus' lectures dealt with cure of the diseases current among the peoples of Europe in the year 1527, and not only did not include comment on the classic medical texts of Galen or Avicenna, an accepted part of every medical lecture worthy of the name, but they attacked these sacrosanct authorities and ridiculed those who followed their teachings. Above all, Paracelsus pled for a medical practice which met the needs of the time, which followed the results of direct observation, and which did away with the ignorance and greed of physicians which hid behind a mask of pompousness and reliance upon the dicta of men who had been dead for centuries.

Paracelsus also was hard at work proving the practical

worth of his knowledge in curing the sick. His success was phenomenal. Maladies previously considered incurable were healed quickly and efficiently by his methods. Case after case which had been given up by other physicians of Basel and the surrounding towns, was brought to him and cured. For two or three years Paracelsus' reputation spread far and wide. Never before had such a physician practiced in Basel!

But this success did not last. At first, his learning, derived from his practical experience, his appeal to the common sense of his hearers, captured the imagination of his students. His successful practice was proof of the correctness of his teaching, and all opposition based on traditionalism was pushed aside.

Slowly, however, the tide began to turn; the waters of opposition gathered their strength. No single detail escaped the vigilant eyes of his enemies; nothing was too insignificant to throw into the scale against him. There was the matter of his having no degree; the conservatives demanded that he be forced to prove his qualifications before continuing his teaching and practice. And his prescriptions were a source of annoyance to the pharmacists of Basel, for Paracelsus had worked out his own system of drug componding, which differed radically from that generally employed by other physicians. Therefore the apothecaries attacked Paracelsus, because he did not use their products as did the Galenists. On the other hand, Paracelsus requested the city authorities to keep close watch on the purity of the drugs sold in Basel, to be certain that the apothecaries really knew their work, and, above all, to be watchful of the commercial relationships between the apothecaries and physicians.

At last the day came for which the enemies of Paracelsus had long been waiting. Among his patients was one Canon Cornelius von Lichtenfels, who had called upon Paracelsus for professional aid when his own physician had given up his case. Although he had promised to pay Paracelsus' fee in the event of a cure, von Lichtenfels now refused to do so. Eventually the matter was taken into a court of law, where the judges found in favor of von Lichtenfels. Noted for his quickness of temper and outspokenness, Paracelsus candidly told the judges his opinion of them, their conduct of the case, and their method of administering the law. When he left the court, Paracelsus' friends advised him to leave Basel without delay, for his enemies would surely see to it that he be severely punished for his speech before the justices. Paracelsus took this advice, and departed from Basel in haste.

Once again Paracelsus resumed his wandering life. For a brief time he remained in Esslingen, then went to Colmar, but the pinch of poverty drove him from town to town in search of work. Twelve years were passed in these journeyings, Paracelsus never remaining in one place for more than a year.

Finally, in 1541 when Paracelsus was forty-eight, he received an invitation which seemed to be the fulfillment of his longing for a permanent home where he could pursue his work undisturbed and in peace. Archbishop Ernst of Salzburg offered Paracelsus his protection if the latter would come to that city and take up his professional activities there.

But Paracelsus was in Salzburg only a few months when he died at almost the same time Michelangelo completed his painting of the "Last Judgment" in the Sistine Chapel at Rome.

Even the reports of Paracelsus' death reflect the efforts of his enemies to defame him. One tale recounts that his death was caused by a drunken brawl in which he was a participant. A report with sinister implications tells that Paracelsus did not die a natural death, but was thrown over a steep cliff at night by assassins in the employ of the apothecaries and physicians, whose vengeance followed him through all his years of exile.

One of Paracelsus' most far-reaching concepts is that of Signatures, that is, the idea that each single part of the microcosmic world of man corresponds with each single part of the macrocosmic world outside man. This leads directly to his teaching concerning Specifics. He realized that the latter were not to be discovered in the labyrinth of often fantastic nostrums and combinations of substances prescribed in the writings of the Galenists. Through careful observation extending over many years, Paracelsus concluded that mineral, plant and animal substances contain within themselves what he called "active principles." It was his conviction that if a method of purification and intensification could be discovered whereby these substances could be caused to release their "active principles," the latter would be infinitely more efficacious and safer in producing a cure than would their crude and often dangerous originals.

Paracelsus died before he could discover the method which could unlock the potency, the healing power latent in mineral, plant and animal substances. This problem was not solved until two and a half centuries later when another physician, Samuel Hahnemann, discovered a method of so handling mineral, plant and animal substances that their innate healing powers were enhanced and made available to a medical practice in line with the highest ideals of cure envisioned by Paracelsus. This method of preparation of substances and the manner of their selection and administration to the sick, Hahnemann called Homeopathy.

The first of Paracelsus' extensive works was published in Augsburg in 1529, memorable as the year when the Reformers' presentation of a protest to the Diet of Spires won them the name of Protestants. Throughout the extensive writings of Paracelsus, repeated again and again in every one of the more than two hundred separate publications of his works which appeared between 1542 and 1845, a single theme is to be observed: The life of man cannot be separated from the life of the universe; therefore, to understand man, understand the universe; to understand the universe, understand man. Only upon such an understanding—universal in its scope—Paracelsus believed a medical art worthy of the name could be built. To the proclamation of such a goal of medicine he devoted his life.

In one of his writings, Paracelsus says, "There is a light in the spirit of man . . . by which the qualities of each thing created by God, whether it be visible or invisible to the senses, may be perceived and known. If man knows the essence of things, their attributes, their attractions, and the elements of which they consist, he will be a master of nature, of the elements, and of the spirits."

Robert Browning expressed Paracelsus' thoughts in the well-known lines:

> "Truth is within ourselves; it takes no rise
> From outward things, what'er you may believe.
> There is an inmost center in us all,
> Where truth abides in fulness; and around,
> Wall upon wall, the gross flesh hems it in,
> This perfect, clear perception—which is truth,
> A baffling and perverting carnal mesh
> Binds it, and makes all error: and, to KNOW,
> Rather consists in opening out a way
> Whence the imprisoned splendor may escape,
> Than in effecting entry for a light
> Supposed to be without."

8.

Eight years before the death of Paracelsus, Valentine Weigel was born at Naundorff, near Grossenheim in the district of Meissen. This year 1533 was also the year of the birth of Montaigne, the skeptic, of the completion of the rape of Peru by the most notorious of all Spanish conquistadores, Francisco Pizarro, of the proclamation of Anne Boleyn, soon to be the mother of Elizabeth, as Queen of England by Henry VIII, and of the final preparation of

Luther's complete German Bible which was published the next year.

The details of Weigel's childhood are obscure, but in course of time he received his Bachelor's and Master's degrees at the University of Leipzig. He continued his studies at the University of Wittenberg until 1567, three years after the death of Michelangelo. In that year he was ordained a Lutheran pastor and was called to the church at Zschopau, not far from Chemnitz in eastern Germany. His life was passed entirely in this place, and he continued as pastor of this church until his death in 1588, the year the English defeated the Spanish Armada.

While the external events of Weigel's life are few and somewhat unimpressive when compared with some of the biographies discussed thus far, his inner development and his dedication to his pastoral tasks are very remarkable. He is remembered as a loving, devoted man, a true shepherd of his flock, a man whom all his parishioners loved, and who loved them in return.

Twenty-one years after the death of their pastor, his parishioners came to know that in addition to the Valentin Weigel they knew, another man, as it were, had been active all the years in Zschopau. This was Valentin Weigel, student, mystic, and author.

Weigel had long been a close student of the writings of Paracelsus, whose work he deeply admired, but whose fate he was determined not to share. Therefore while he studied and wrote a great deal during his lifetime, he never revealed his interest in mysticism to anyone, and left instructions that his writings were not to be published until sometime after his death. So while Pastor Weigel stood in his pulpit and preached to his flock Sunday after Sunday without interruption for twenty-one years, he never shared his most cherished interests and convictions with them.

Weigel was well acquainted with the works of Eckhart and Tauler and also with such classical mystics as Dionysius and the Neo-Platonists. But with all his study he recognized that the ultimate truth of things is not acquired from without, but is to be found within each man. He wrote, "Study nature, physics, alchemy, magic, and so on, but *it is all in you*, and you become what you have learned."

In 1609, twenty-one years after Weigel's death, the year Henry Hudson sailed up the river that now bears his name, Weigel's book that was to greatly influence English mystics after its translation into English in 1648, was published. It bore the title, *Von den Leben Christi, das ist, vom wahren Glauben,* Of the Life of Christ, that is, of True Faith, and one of its outstanding passages is, "Faith comes by inward hearing. Good books, external preaching, have their place; they testify to the real Treasure. They are witnesses to the Word within us. But faith is not tied to books; Faith is *a new birth,* which cannot be found in books. The one who has the inner Schoolmaster would lose nothing of his salvation, even though all the preachers should die and all books be burned."

When one considers the theological ideas prevailing in his time, one of Weigel's interesting concepts deals with the location of heaven and hell. In an age when basically materialistic descriptions of heavenly wonders were contrasted with equally materialistic portrayals of hellish tortures, and men were assured by their pastors that these were definite *places,* Weigel's conviction, which probably he never voiced from his pulpit, is surprisingly modern. He wrote that "Heaven and Hell are in the soul of man, after all; both Trees of the Paradise, the Tree of Knowledge of Good and Evil, as well as the Tree of Life, flourish in the human soul." (See Weigel's *Erkenne dich Selbst,* Know Thyself)

Like Luther and others, Weigel prized and edited the little book, *Theologia Germanica,* or *The Golden Book of German Theology,* as Henry More called it, and spoke of it as "A precious little book, a noble book." Weigel also loved the sermons of Johannes Tauler because "they testify to the experience of the Heavenly Jerusalem within us."

For Weigel, the immanence of the spiritual world was a profound conviction, born of his personal experience. His expression of this is one of the classic statements of mysticism: "God is nearer to us than we are to ourselves."

9.

Jacob Boehme was born on April 24, 1575 in the little German village of Alt Seidenberg on a hillside south of Goerlitz, near the Bohemian border. Jacob was the fourth child of his parents, of old German peasant stock, noted for their honesty and devoutness. The Boehme family were staunch Lutherans, and the children were brought up according to the family faith. Jacob was a sickly child, and was not thought strong enough to work in the fields. Therefore his childhood summers were spent watching the herds, and in winter he received the rudiments of reading, writing, simple arithmetic and a little Latin. His favorite reading was his Bible, which he carried with him in the fields, and came to know as few other men have.

When he was fourteen, his father apprenticed him to the village cobbler for three years, since it was clear that Jacob's health would never permit him to be a farmer. In 1592 Jacob Boehme began his journeyman's wanderings.

Abraham von Franckenberg, whom we shall meet again as the friend of Johannes Scheffler (Angelus Silesius), knew Jacob Boehme, and described the latter's appearance in these years: "Jacob's body was worn and plain. He was short, with low forehead, wide temples, his nose slightly crooked, his eyes grey, lighting up at times like the windows of Solomon's Temple. He had a short beard, somewhat thin, a slight voice, but very gentle in conversation. His manner was modest, mild and humble. He was of patient heart, and his spirit was lightened by God beyond anything to be found in nature."

In the chapter in this book dealing with Jacob Boehme, Rudolf Steiner relates the famous story of the stranger and the pair of shoes, which took place during Boehme's apprentice days, sometime before 1599. In May of that year Boehme was officially made a citizen of Goerlitz, became established as a master shoemaker there, and soon afterward married Catherina Kuntzsch, daughter of a butcher of Goerlitz, by whom he had four children.

In the year 1600, when Jacob Boehme was twenty-five,

he had the remarkable spiritual experience which Rudolf Steiner mentions in this book. Boehme saw the sunlight reflected on the surface of a polished pewter dish, and it was suddenly as though he could penetrate into the most secret depths of the universe, could probe the secrets of nature, and could fathom the essential being of everything in creation. This is comparable to Paracelsus' observation: "Hidden things which cannot be perceived by the physical senses may be discovered by means of the sidereal body, through whose organism we can look into nature just as the sun shines through a glass."

Boehme later explained his spiritual experience or "illumination" in the introduction to his book, *Aurora:* "In a quarter of an hour I observed and knew more than if I had attended a university for many years. I recognized the Being of Beings, both the Byss and Abyss, the eternal generation of the Trinity, the origin and creation of this world and of all creatures through the Divine Wisdom. I saw all three worlds in myself: first, the Divine World; second, the dark world and the source of fire; third, the external, visible world as an outbreathing of the inner or spiritual worlds. I also saw the fundamental nature of evil and good, and how the pregnant Mother, the eternal genetrix, brought them forth. My experience is like the evoking of life in the presence of death, or like the resurrection from the dead. My spirit suddenly saw all created things, even the herbs and grass, in this light. I knew who God is, what He is like, and the nature of His Will. Suddenly in that light my will was seized by a mighty impulse to describe the Being of God."

For ten long years after this spiritual experience, to which Boehme referred repeatedly throughout the remainder of his life, he meditated on his vision. He came to believe that what he had to tell others was entirely unique with him, and that his mission was to purify Christianity, which he thought had become corrupt once again. He had no use for theology born of reason, nor for creeds and dogmas established on purely intellctual foundations. He was convinced that only one's personal experience of the reality of the spiritual world can enable one to overcome evil and advance into genuine knowledge of the spirit.

In 1610, the year when Galileo discovered the satellites of Jupiter by means of the newly-invented telescope, Jacob Boehme knew that the moment had come when he could write down an account of what he had seen a decade before: "To write these things was strongly urged upon my spirit, however difficult they might be for my outer self to understand, and for my pen to express. Like a child beginning school I was compelled to start my work on this very great Mystery. Within myself I saw it well enough, as in a great depth, but the describing and explaining of it seemed impossible."

Boehme wrote in the early morning before he went to his cobbler's bench, and in the evening after he returned home from his work. And at last, after two years of diligent effort, Jacob Boehme produced his *Aurora*, one of the masterpieces of mystical literature.

That Boehme knew that the twenty-six chapters of his *Aurora* are not easy to read, and are not for everyman, is

clear from his words: "If you are not a spiritual over-
comer, then let my book alone. Don't meddle with it, but
stick to your old ways." "Art was not written here, nor
did I find time to consider how to set things down accu-
rately, according to rules of composition, but everything
followed the direction of the Spirit, which often hastened
so that the writer's hand shook. As the burning fire of the
Spirit hurried ahead, the hand and pen had to follow after
it, for it came and went like a sudden shower."

Handwritten copies of the manuscript were made by
Carl Ender von Sercha, Boehme's friend and student.
Sercha believed that in Boehme's work a prophecy of
Paracelsus had been fulfilled, which announced that the
years between 1599 and 1603 would bring about a new
age for mankind, a time of "singing, dancing, rejoicing,
jubilating." Therefore many who heard of Boehme's remarkable spiritual experience when he had, to use his
own words, "wrestled in God's presence a considerable
time for the knightly crown . . . which later, with the
breaking of the gate in the deep center of nature, I attained with much joy," believed that in him the words of
Paracelsus had come true.

Their enthusiasm, however, was not universally shared.
A copy of the manuscript of *Aurora* fell by chance into
the hands of the Lutheran Pastor Primarius Gregorius
Richter of Goerlitz. After the clergyman read the pages
that John Wesley was later to describe as "sublime non-
sense, inimitable bombast, fustian not to be paralleled,"
and the celebrated English Bishop Warburton characterized as something that "would disgrace Bedlam at full

moon," he went to his pulpit the next Sunday and poured
out his indignation upon Boehme's work. Among the congregation that morning sat Jacob Boehme himself, who
listened quietly and without a shadow of emotion to the
stern denunciations of his pastor. Afterward he went to
Richter and attempted to explain the passages of *Aurora*
to which the latter took most violent exception. But the
clergyman would have neither Boehme nor his book, and
asked the town council to expel Boehme from Goerlitz.
His effort failed, but the justices warned Boehme that
since he was a shoemaker, he must abandon writing and
stick to the trade for which he was licensed. Boehme, who
had said, "In Yes and No all things consist," accepted
their injunction, and entered upon still another time of
silence. This period lasted from 1612, the year the King
James Version of the English Bible was issued, until 1619,
when a Dutch ship landed in Jamestown, Virginia, with
the first African slaves to be sold in North America.

Meanwhile, Boehme's fame was spreading as more and
more people read the manuscript copies of his *Aurora,*
which were circulated by his admirers. Among the latter
were the physician of Goerlitz, the learned Dr. Tobias
Kober, the director of the Elector of Saxony's chemical
laboratory at Dresden, Dr. Balthazar Walther, the nobleman Carl Ender von Sercha, and the Paracelsus student,
who was to be Boehme's biographer, Abraham von
Franckenberg.

Again and again these men urged Boehme to ignore the
order of the magistrates of Goerlitz, and to continue his
writing, but he consistently refused. However, early in

1619 their urgings met with success, and Boehme resumed his writing, and continued with increasing zeal during the following years. As he wrote, "I had resolved to do nothing in future, but to be quiet before God in obedience, and to let the devil with all his host sweep over me. But with me it was as when a seed is hidden in the earth. Contrary to all reason, it grows up in storm and rough weather. In the winter, all is dead, and reason says, 'Everything is ended for it.' But the precious seed within me sprouted and grew green, oblivious of all storms, and, amid disgrace and ridicule, it has blossomed into a lily!"

Through all the following years Boehme remained faithful to his original conviction that everything he wrote was not the fruit of his own intellectual creativeness, but was the gift of the spiritual world. In 1620, the memorable year of the Pilgrim Fathers at Plymouth, he said, "I did not dare to write other than as I was guided. I have continued writing as the Spirit directed, and have not given place to reason."

Boehme was one of those people who suffer much from the enthusiasm and admiration of their friends. The latter were responsible for the attack by Pastor Primarius Richter, because of their circulating copies of *Aurora,* as we have seen. Again, toward the end of 1623, Boehme's friend, Sigismund von Schweinitz published three small works of Boehme, the first of the latter's writings to appear in print. Immediately the enemy in the person of clergyman Richter attacked Jacob Boehme, and once again complained to the magistrates of Goerlitz. This time, since he had broken their injunction against his writing, they ordered Boehme to leave town.

Before receiving the sentence of the magistrates, however, Boehme had been invited to visit the Court of the Elector of Saxony in Dresden. Therefore, early in May the shoemaker-exile from Goerlitz arrived in Dresden to attend "a conference of noble people," as he described it.

Boehme was fast becoming famous. The second attack upon him by Pastor Primarius Richter was known widely, and the sale of his writings, which were rapidly appearing in print, steadily increased. He was convinced that in only a short time "the nations will take up what my native town is casting away." He regarded the invitation to the Elector's Court as an opportunity to defend his works before some of the leading theologians and scholars of his time, and he was right.

His devoted student, Dr. Balthasar Walther, had arranged that Boehme was to be a guest in the home of Dr. Benedict Hinckelmann, Walther's successor as director of the Elector's laboratory, and the court physician. Boehme's reception in Dresden was all that his most devoted friends could have desired. He was entertained with consideration and appreciation, and found that important members of the court circle had studied his writings, and welcomed this opportunity to discuss them with him. One of the prominent noblemen of the Elector's household, Joachim von Loss, invited Boehme to visit his castle in order that they might have conversation together. Major Stahlmeister, chief master of horse to the Elector, did everything possible to inform the Elector favorably concerning Boehme's work.

Finally, at the request of the Elector, Boehme was examined orally by six eminently learned doctors of theology, and by two mathematicians. As a contemporary account describes it, "The illustrious Elector found great satisfaction in Boehme's answers. He asked Boehme to come to him privately, spoke with him, extended many favors to him, and gave him permission to return to his home in Goerlitz."

At the conclusion of his visit, which lasted nearly two months, Boehme left Dresden, his teachings at least partly accepted. He did not return directly to Goerlitz, but visited three of his noblemen friends on the way. At the home of one of them he was taken ill, and as soon as possible, he hastened home to Goerlitz, where his friend and physician, Dr. Tobias Kober undertook his care. It was not long, however, before Dr. Kober, realizing that Jacob Boehme's death was near, arranged that he should receive the sacrament of the Lord's Supper after he had made a confession of faith. This was done on November 15, 1624.

It was nearly two o'clock in the morning of the following Sunday that Jacob Boehme asked his son, Tobias, "Do you hear that beautiful music, my son?" Tobias replied that he did not. Then Boehme said, "Open the door then, so we can hear it better." He inquired as to the hour, and when he was told that it was not yet three oclock, he replied, "Then my time has not yet come."

With the first faint touches of Aurora on the eastern sky, Jacob Boehme spoke words of farewell to his wife and children, and with a smile of joyful expectancy on his face, breathed out his spirit with the words, "Now I go to Paradise!"

A great crowd of the everyday people of Goerlitz, the shoemakers, tanners, craftsmen, along with devoted students of Boehme's writings, attended his funeral. The pall-bearers were shoemakers of Goerlitz, and the funeral service was conducted by the Lutheran clergyman who succeeded Richter. On the tombstone of porphry are inscribed the words, "Jacob Boehme, *philosophus Teutonicus.*"

Jacob Boehme once described life as "a curious bath of thorns and thistles," and his experience witnessed the truth of his words. But all the difficulties of his comparatively short life of forty-nine years were more than compensated by his vision of the greatness of man and of man's destiny. As he wrote, "Man has a spark of the spirit as a supernatural gift of God, to bring forth by degrees a new birth of that life which was lost in Paradise. This sacred spark of the divine nature within man has a natural, strong, almost infinite longing for that eternal spirit of God from which it came forth. It came forth from God, it came out of God; therefore it is always in a state of return to God. All this is called the breathing, the quickening of the Holy Spirit within us, which are so many operations of this spark of life, tending toward God."

10.

In 1548, the year Michelangelo was made chief archi-
tect of St. Peter's in Rome, Giordano Bruno was born
beneath the shadow of Mount Vesuvius in the little village of Cicala near Nola. His boyhood was passed in the
midst of earthquakes, plagues and famine, while robbers
and outlaws frequented the hills and fields of his native
countryside. His father was a soldier, and the boy was
named Philip.

At the age of fifteen he was enrolled in the Dominican
monastery in Naples, the same cloister where Thomas
Aquinas had lived three hundred years before. There he
was given the name Giordano, which had been the name
of one of the intimate companions of St. Dominic himself.

For nearly thirteen years he studied in this monastery,
and became learned in the works of the ancient philosophers, particularly of Plotinus and Pythagoras. He was
of an independent spirit, and gave considerable concern
to his censor on this account. For example, he removed
the saints' pictures from his cell, leaving only the crucifix
on the wall. When he discovered a monk reading *The
Seven Joys of Mary,* he advised him to read something
more rational. He also questioned points in the Church
dogma such as the Transsubstantiation, the Trinity, and
the Immaculate Conception. At an early age he was deeply
impressed with the scientific writings of Copernicus, and
after some twenty years of reading them recalled that the
force of their teaching still worked strongly upon him.

The teachings of the Neo-Platonists and of Nicolas of

Cusa formed the basis of his own philosophy, and during his early years he wrote considerable poetry as well.

In 1572, when Bruno was twenty-four, he took holy orders, read his first Mass, and began to perform the other priestly functions. About this time he took some of his companions into his confidence, and frankly told them some of the questions he entertained on matters of Church dogma. They lost no time in informing their superiors, and soon the Holy Office of the Inquisition reprimanded Bruno sharply. Plans were made to bring him before a court of the Inquisition, but Bruno secretly left Naples and went to Rome, where he stayed in the Della Minerva Monastery.

However, he was not long left in peace. Fra Domenico Vito, provincial of the Order, charged him with heresy, and orders for his arrest were sent to Rome. Letters from friends informed Bruno that soon after his departure from Naples his books which he had hidden, had been discovered, including works by Chrisostom and Hieronymous, with notes by Erasmus. Bruno's situation was very serious, and he left the monastery, divested himself of his Dominican habit, and wandered over the Campagna in the vicinity of the ruins of Hadrian's villa dressed as a poor beggar, which indeed he was. These events occurred in 1576-1577, at about the time of the birth of the painter, Peter Paul Rubens.

Now began Bruno's years of wandering, during which he sought to make known the new teachings about the universe as set forth by Copernicus. He also continued his own writings, creating philosophical masterpieces and poetic works of unusual mystical depth and content. He took passage in a ship bound for Genoa, but was unable to land because of the plague and civil war. Therefore he stopped at Noli, on the Riviera, where he taught boys grammar and delivered lectures on the work of Copernicus, the plurality of worlds, and the shape of the earth. But this was too much for the local clergy, and once again Bruno wandered to Turin, where he hoped to obtain an opportunity to lecture in the University through the celebrated patron of scholars, Duke Emmanuele Filberto. However, the latter was under the influence of the Jesuits, and once again Bruno was denied the post he sought.

Bruno reached Venice after traveling across northern Italy from Turin, but here too he found that the deadly plague had done its work as in Genoa, and a large part of the inhabitants—including the painter Titian at the age of ninety-nine—had died. However, Venice was the center of the publishing activities of Italy, and Bruno braved the plague in order to have some of his work printed there. Shortly afterward he visited the Dominicans at Padua, and "they persuaded me to wear the habit again, even though I would not profess the religion it implied, because they said it would help in my travels to be thus dressed. And so I put on the white cloth robe and the hood which I had kept by me when I left Rome."

When Bruno arrived in Geneva, the Marchese Galcazzo Carraciola, nephew of Pope Paul IV, also a refugee from persecution by the church, and a member of the Calvinist Protestant religion, befriended him. The Marchese asked him to cease wearing the Dominican habit and to assume the usual dress of the lay scholar, and Bruno did so, never again wearing a religious habit. During his stay in Geneva, Bruno found himself in trouble with Antoine de la Faye, a member of the Academy, because he took exception to one of the latter's lectures, and attacked some twenty points in it. Bruno was arrested and imprisoned for a short time, and after his release was informed that he must either adopt Calvinism or leave the city.

Shortly after this Bruno entered France, visting Lyons and afterwards Toulouse. In the latter place he received his Doctor's degree, and held the position of professor of philosophy in the university for two years, lecturing to appreciative hearers on astronomy and general philosophical subjects. But again the clergy interfered with his work, and he left Toulouse for Paris, where he arrived in 1581.

Henry III, king of France, had heard of Bruno's great gifts as a lecturer, and of his unusual learning, eloquence and memory. Therefore he wished to appoint Bruno to the faculty of the Sorbonne, but before doing so, it was necessary for Bruno to confess and attend Mass as a professing Catholic. Bruno fearlessly and uncompromisingly refused, and so greatly did his honesty and sincerity impress the king that the latter allowed him to assume the position without regard to his scruples concerning religion.

The Paris lectures of Giordano Bruno were based on his study of the famous treatise, the *Ars Magna*, which Raimon Lull, the eminent Majorcan author, Arabic scholar, mystic, educational reformer, and traveller, had written in 1275. In addition, Bruno discussed logic, general philosophy, astronomy, the symbolism of Pythagoras, and the teachings of Copernicus.

After two years' teaching in Paris, Bruno was offered the post of secretary to Michel de Castelnau, sieur de Mauvissière, ambassador to England. Bruno found London in a ferment of excitement, since attempts had recently been made on the life of Queen Elizabeth. Added to this were constant rumors that the Spanish were preparing to launch a massive invasion attempt against the coasts of England, and after Bruno had been in England for about a year, these rumors were confirmed by accurate information that a great Armada was gathering in the Tagus with designs upon England.

But politics, rumors of invasion, and tales of military exploit did not interest Bruno. He visited Oxford, and was disappointed with what he found there. From the time he first landed in the country, he had been repelled by what he considered the brutality of English manners in contrast with those he had known in Italy and France. In Protestant Oxford Bruno found a narrowness and sectarian dogmatism entirely foreign to the ideas of objective freedom he believed should prevail among scholars. The presence of the distinguished Polish Prince Johann a Lesco at Oxford was the occasion for a debate in which Bruno defended his new cosmology based on the teachings of the Polish Copernicus, against a group of theologians. Bruno won easily, but was soon forbidden to continue his lectures in Oxford.

While Bruno found the manners of the British distasteful, and the attitude of the Oxford scholars hopelessly bigoted, in the person of the Queen he found something to admire. He was frequently invited to private conversations with Elizabeth, who was always happy when she could display her knowledge of Italian, and who appreciated Bruno's learning and charm. In London, Bruno met the brilliant statesman, Sir Philip Sydney, to whom he dedicated one of his works, Lord Bacon of Verulam, and other prominent figures of the Elizabethan court. Bruno's duties at the embassy apparently were not arduous, since he seems to have had time to mingle with the court, to form acquaintances with the leading men of the time (there is a tradition that he met Shakespeare in the printing shop of Thomas Vautrollier), to hold lectures at Oxford, and—most important for posterity—to devote himself to writing.

In 1584 while Sir Walter Raleigh's expedition in Virginia was taking place, and the plot involving Mary Queen of Scots was fast coming to a head, Bruno wrote his two most famous metaphysical works, *De la Causa, Principio, ed Uno,* and *D l'Infinito, Universo, e Mondi.*

Early in 1585, with the plans for an English invasion of the Netherlands taking shape, and the raids on the Spanish American coasts by Sir Francis Drake making certain a crisis with Spain, the French ambassador decided he should return to France for a time. Therefore Bruno left England, probably not too unwillingly, though the years of his English residence were among the most productive and happiest of his life.

Bruno's ideas were found acceptable to the superiors of the college of Cambrai, and he found a temporary place among the lecturers there. However, his outspokenness brought him into trouble, for he prepared a thesis of one hundred twenty articles, in which he attacked the philosophy of Aristotle. His works and teaching evoked enthusiasm such as had not been witnessed in academic circles in France since the times of Abèlard. Bruno's theses were printed by permission of the censor, and the debate on them was held on May 25, 1588, at Whitsuntide.

At once after his triumph, Bruno left France for Germany, where he hoped to find freedom to lecture. In Marburg he was disappointed, but in Wittenberg he was welcomed, and found the atmosphere congenial to his creative activity. There he produced several more written works.

In 1588, with Europe ablaze with the tale of the defeat of the Spanish Armada, and with it the hope of Philip II to crush English Protestantism under the tread of invading Spanish Catholic armies, Bruno decided to visit Prague. From there he went to the university at Helmstadt where he remained for a year, but at the end of that time was driven out by the attacks of Boethius, Lutheran Rector of Helmstadt. Bruno decided to go to Frankfort, where he hoped to prepare and publish several works, but he was not allowed to enter the city. Instead he found refuge in a Carmelite cloister just outside the city, through the kind assistance of the famous publishers, Wechel and Fischer. In the cloister he worked with feverish haste, and produced a number of works which were published. The

Prior of the monastery recalled Bruno as "a man of universal mind, skillful in all sciences, but without a trace of religion."

During this period—when he wrote his *Seven Liberal Arts*—the Frankfort Fair took place, and many publishers from foreign countries were present. There Bruno met the Venetian booksellers, Bertano and Ciotto, and it was the latter who took Bruno's writings to Venice. There these were found by a young nobleman, Giovanni Mocenigo, who read them with great interest, and inquired for details about the author.

Sometime later, when Bruno was in Zürich a letter reached him from the young Mocenigo, inviting him to visit him in Venice, promising him safe conduct for the journey. As soon as Bruno's friends heard of the invitation, they urged him not to accept it, for they feared for his safety at the hands of the Inquisition. But Bruno brushed their fears aside. He had confidence in this young nobleman, a member of one of the finest and most honorable families of Venice. Therefore, Bruno crossed the Alps and descended into Italy, arriving in Venice in October, 1591.

The first months after Bruno's arrival were filled with scholarly activity. He began to tutor the young Mocenigo, and also lectured privately to German students at Padua, where he was soon to be followed by Galileo. Bruno frequented the Venetian philosophical and literary societies, and was welcomed in the home of Andrea Morosini and of his student Mocenigo. Finally, after some time Bruno decided that he would like to return to Frankfort in order to publish some of his works there. But this was not to be.

From the moment he had arrived in Italy the spies of the Inquisition were on his track, and Giovanni Mocenigo cooperated with them. And now that Bruno wished to leave the country, Mocenigo had him arrested, and thrown into the prison of the Inquistion. He was charged with many heresies, most serious being his teaching of the infinity of the universe.

Bruno was kept in the prison at Venice for nine months, and at the end of that time was taken in chains to the Bridge of Sighs, and was conveyed through the lagoons to Ancona, where he remained until he was taken to Rome. After torture and solitary confinement at Ancona, Bruno was turned over to the Roman Inquisition, and for seven years he experienced the terrors of the prison of the Holy Office. To the last he refused to give up his beliefs, and defied his opponents in all they brought against him. On February 9, 1600 Bruno was excommunicated with the cries of "Anathema."

On February 16th in the Campo dei Fiori, a Roman flower market, Giordano Bruno was burned at the stake. He was hardly fifty years of age, and his body showed signs of dreadful torture. With his head erect, his eyes showing full consciousness, he walked unassisted to the stake.

Rudolf Steiner said in a lecture on January 12, 1923, "The flaming pyre in which Giordano Bruno was put to death in the year 1600 was an outer sign of a most significant phase of inner development. . . . The flames in Rome are a glorious memorial in history, as Giordano

Bruno himself indicated. While he was burning, he said, Something *will* come into being. And what was destined to come into being, what drew forth the cry, You can put me to death, but not through centuries will my ideas be able to be put to death,—that is precisely what must live on."

11.

Shortly after the beginning of the Thirty Years' War, in the year Virginia became a royal colony, with governor and council appointed by the British crown, and two years after New Netherlands was established as a Dutch colony in America, Johannes Scheffler was born in the German city of Breslau in Silesia, in 1624, the year Jacob Boehme died. When Johannes was five, his mother enrolled him and his brother at the Elizabeth Gymnasium in Breslau, shortly before her death. At the age of nineteen Johannes Scheffler matriculated at the University of Strassburg, where he intended to study medicine and law. After a year at Strassburg, he entered the University of Leyden and remained there two years. While he was at Leyden Scheffler discovered the works of Jacob Boehme, which had been published at Amsterdam in 1642. As he expressed it, "When one is in Holland, all sorts of things come one's way."

From Leyden, Scheffler went to the greatest medical school at that time, the University of Padua, where he received his degree of Doctor of Medicine and Philosophy in 1648.

At about this time he wrote in the album of one of his fellow students, *Mundus nihil pulcherrimum,* The world is a very beautiful Nothing. In 1649 Johannes Scheffler was appointed Court physician to the strict Lutheran Duke Sylvanus Nimrod at Oels in Württemberg. Shortly before Scheffler arrived in Oels, the town of four thousand inhabitants had been reduced to less than two thousand, due to an action which had been fought there in the Thirty Years' War. The cattle had been killed, crops destroyed, houses ruined, and even the castle of the Duke was slightly damaged.

At the same time that Scheffler came to Oels, an older man also arrived in the town. He had been born there fifty-six years before, and was destined to play an important role in the life of Scheffler. This man was Abraham von Franckenberg, whom we have already met as the friend and biographer of Boehme; as Scheffler's friend he was to guide the latter on his spiritual path.

Years before, von Franckenberg had given over his estate to his eldest son, and had reserved only two small rooms in the house for himself, where he studied and lived. During the plagues which swept over the district from time to time, he was of great help to the sick. It was at a time of plague that he met Jacob Boehme, and eventually printed the latter's writings at his own expense. Von Franckenberg studied Kaballa, alchemy, the works of Giordano Bruno and Copernicus, with the single aim of solving the secrets of the science of nature. Because of his studies von Franckenberg was attacked by the Lutheran clergy, and finally left Oels in 1641, and went to Danzig where he lived for eight years as the guest of the famous astronomer, Helvelius. From Danzig he returned to Oels in 1649. When he was asked by the Duke if he was a Catholic, a Lutheran, or a Calvinist, von Franckenberg answered, "I am the heart of all these religions."

Johannes Scheffler was attracted to von Franckenberg at their first meeting, and soon the young physician became the devoted student of the older scientist. Long hours were spent by the two of them in von Franckenberg's little rooms discussing Boehme, alchemy, astronomy, the mystics of medieval times, and so on. Two and one-half years after their meeting, von Franckenberg died, and bequeathed many of his precious books and manuscripts to Scheffler. Among these works, which Scheffler referred to as "a real pharmacy of the soul," were the *Theologia Germanica,* the writings of Boehme, Weigel, Paracelsus, Bruno, Tauler and Rulwin Merswin. One volume of this collection is preserved, and bears the date 1652 inscribed on the flyleaf, and in the handwriting of Scheffler, the words, "From my faithful friend, Abraham von Franckenberg." Another volume from this collection also contains extensive notations in Scheffler's handwriting.

Shortly after von Franckenberg's death, Scheffler decided to write a book composed of passages from his favorite mystical authors. This he intended to issue as a New Year gift volume. As a matter of course the printer submitted the book to Christoph Freytag, court chaplain and censor. Freytag struck out long passages, and not only refused to give his imprimatur, but also declined to so much as speak with Scheffler about it. This was a turning-point in Scheffler's spiritual life. He realized that the Lutheran church could no longer be his religious home. He resigned his post, left Oels immediately, and returned to Breslau.

Among the writers whom Scheffler had quoted in his book, many were Catholic. Now he began to read Catholic books more and more, spending some months in Breslau in thorough study of them. On June 12, 1653 Johannes Scheffler embraced the Roman Catholic faith.

As Abraham von Franckenberg had been a strong influence in Scheffler's life at one point, now a second man exerted a powerful effect upon him. This was Sebastian von Rostock, born the son of a poor ropemaker, now the vicar general of the diocese of Breslau. As a simple parish priest in the village of Niesse he had witnessed the hardships of the Thirty Years' War. For example, when the Lutheran armies rounded up many Catholics and imprisoned them in buildings, he risked his life by climbing in the windows to give them spiritual consolation. One day while he was walking through the forest, he was set upon by a Lutheran cavalryman. He drew his sword, which all men, clergymen or not had to wear at that time for self-protection, returned the attack, and killed his opponent. However, the instant the cavalryman fell from his horse, von Rostock rushed to him in order to give him absolution that he might die in a state of grace. In the Catholic Counter-Reformation of 1653-4, von Rostock was extremely severe on the Lutherans, with the result that over two hundred fifty churches were returned to Catholic use in Silesia alone.

At this point, however, von Rostock wished to have some proof that Lutherans were finding it possible to embrace the Catholic faith without pressure or force.

Therefore the free conversion of the celebrated former court physician, Johannes Scheffler, was precisely the example he was looking for. He sought out Scheffler, who by this time had decided to change his name. First he adopted the name of Johannes de Angelis, a Spanish mystic of the sixteenth century, calling himself Johannes Angelus. But he discovered that there existed a certain Protestant doctor of theology, Johannes Angelus of Darmstadt, so he added "Silesius" from his birthplace, calling himself Johannes Angelus Silesius, by which he is known to posterity.

Sebastian von Rostock invited Angelus Silesius to his palace, and after talking with him arranged that the Austrian Emperor, Frederick III would give him the title of Court physician, but without either duties or salary. Nevertheless the title alone gave Angelus Silesius good reputation in Catholic circles particularly. More important, however, is the fact that von Rostock give his imprimatur to Angelus Silesius' *Geistreiche Sinn und Schlussreime*, Witty Sayings and End-Rhymes, which, when it was reprinted in 1674 was given the name by which it has since become famous, *Cherubinischer Wandersmann*, The Cherubinean Wanderer. The book was approved in July, 1656, but was not published until 1657, the year before the birth of the English composer, Henry Purcell. In 1674 Angelus Silesius' collection of some two hundred poems was published under the title, *Heilige Seelenlust, oder geistliche Hirtenlieder der in ihren Jesum verliebten Psyche*, Holy Ecstasies, or Sacred Shepherd Songs in Adoration of Jesus. From this collection, several poems were eventually included in the Lutheran hymnal, and today are among the best-loved hymns of the Protestant church.

Angelus Silesius became extremely zealous in developing the activities of the Catholic church in Breslau. Now a Franciscan priest, he organized the first Catholic procession held in Breslau for well over a century. And to drive the lesson home to observers, Angelus Silesius himself carried the cross and wore the crown of thorns in the procession. The next twelve years were a period of intense controversy, for in that time Angelus Silesius wrote and published some fifty-five attacks on Protestantism, most of them extremely bitter. Finally he was persuaded to give up this activity by the superior of his Order.

In 1664 Angelus Silesius was appointed marshal and counsellor to Sebastian von Rostock, who meanwhile had become Prince-Bishop of Breslau. Seven years later the Prince-Bishop died suddenly, and a sadness settled upon Angelus Silesius which did not leave him until death.

Just as Sebastian von Rostock had appeared after the death of Abraham von Franckenberg, now a third man befriended Angelus Silesius. This was Bernard Rose, Abbot of the Cistercian monastery of Grüssau, and Vicar General of the Cistercians in Silesia. Abbot Rose was a man of great strength, kindness of heart, a stern disciplinarian in his monastery, and a firm supporter of the Counter-Reformation. The monastery of Grüssau was located about fifty miles from Breslau, and was noted for its hospitality to all who knocked at its gates.

Angelus Silesius was received with warmth and kindliness at Grüssau. He found understanding, support, and comfort, of inestimable value to him, since now he was a dying man. The months he lived at Grüssau were spent in writing, meditation, and prayer. There he completed his last work, the *Ecclesiologia*, which he dedicated to Abbot Bernard Rose, his friend. The last three months of Angelus Silesius' life were marked by severe suffering, but through it all he was able to maintain an attitude of inner calm, of lofty spiritual vision, and of clear consciousness. He died on July 9, 1677, and to the last moment of his life he never ceased to manifest the spirit of love and peace which had settled upon him during his severe illness. In his last days Angelus Silesius repeated again and again, "Tranquillity is the best treasure that one can have."

*

In the Loggia di San Paolo on the south side of the square, opposite the Church of Santa Maria Novella in Florence is a famous terra cotta relief created by Andrea della Robbia sometime around 1492. Influenced by a work of Fra Angelico, it depicts the historic meeting between St. Francis and St. Dominic. When one contemplates what is represented there, one is reminded of the Scripture, "Mercy and truth are met together." An Italian, whose life-work was centered in a love which is ever merciful, embraces a Spaniard, whose striving for truth was expressed in knowledge of the eternal spirit.

Rudolf Steiner once observed that "External events, which at first glance seem to be trifling occurrences in the course of history, are deeply and inwardly rooted in the evolution of mankind."

In this sense, this artistic creation, fashioned at the moment of emergence of the modern world, portraying the meeting of the founders of two great streams of spiritual aspiration which arose in the Middle Ages, bearing the classic Platonic and Aristotelian impulses into later times, expresses their significance in the development of mankind.

The series of eleven men around whom this book is created, begins with Meister Eckhart, a Dominican, and concludes with Angelus Silesius, a Franciscan. Midway between the two Rudolf Steiner places Henry Cornelius, Agrippa of Nettesheim, typical of the "new man" of the Renaissance: scholar, courtier, diplomat, physician, master of the "new learning" which came to the fore at the dawn of the modern age. Between the Dominicans, for whom the ideal picture of the world was embodied in the word Order, and the Franciscans, for whom the essence of creation was expressed in the word Love, Rudolf Steiner has placed the figure whom he calls "a protagonist for a genuine science of nature."

In the lives of these eleven men is united the progressive unfoldment of ideas and events at a moment of supreme importance in the course of man's life on earth. Their struggles, tensions, and resolutions epitomize the historical process as it unveiled itself in the important development then taking place in the evolution of humanity. In their life-experiences we see the birth-pangs of the appearance of a new stage in the life of mankind—the dawn of the modern age.　　PAUL MARSHALL ALLEN

Alvastra,
South Egremont, Massachusetts
August, 1960

PREFACE TO THE 1923 EDITION

IN THIS WORK more than twenty years ago, I wanted to answer the question, Why do a particular form of mysticism and the beginnings of modern scientific thinking clash in a period from the thirteenth to the seventeenth century.

I did not wish to write a "history" of the mysticism of this period, but only to answer this question. The publications which have appeared on this subject in the past twenty years do not, in my opinion, furnish any grounds for making any changes in the answer. The work can therefore reappear in the main unchanged.

The mystics who are dealt with here are the last offshoots of a way of inquiry and thinking which in its details is foreign to present-day consciousness. However, the disposition of soul which lived in this way of inquiry exists in thoughtful natures at the present time. The manner of looking at objects of nature with which, before the period characterized here, this disposition of soul was connected, has almost disappeared. Its place has been taken by present-day natural science.

The personalities described in this book were not able to transmit the earlier way of inquiry to the future. It no longer corresponds to the cognitive powers which have developed in European man from the thirteenth and fourteenth century onward. What Paracelsus or Jacob Boehme preserve of this way of inquiry appears only as a reminiscence of something past. In essense it is the disposition of soul which remains to thoughtful men. And for it they seek an impulse in the inclinations of the soul itself, while formerly it arose in the soul when the latter observed nature. Many of those who incline toward mysticism today do not want to kindle mystical experiences in connection with what present-day natural science says, but with what the works of the period described here contain. But in this way they become strangers to what most occupies the present.

It might appear as though the present-day knowledge of nature, seen in its true character, does not indicate a way which could so incline the soul as to find, in mystical contemplation, the light of the spirit. Why do mystically inclined souls find satisfaction in Meister Eckhart, in Jacob Boehme, etc., but not in the book of nature, insofar as, opened by knowledge, it lies before man today?

It is true that the manner in which this book of nature is discussed today for the most part, cannot lead to a mystical disposition of soul.

It is the intention of this work to indicate that this manner of discussion does not have to be used. This is attempted by speaking also of those spirits who, out of the disposition of soul of the old mysticism, developed a way of thinking which also can incorporate the newer knowledge into itself. This is the case with Nicolas of Cusa.

In such personalities it becomes apparent that present-day natural science too is capable of a mystical intensification. For a Nicolas of Cusa would be able to lead his thinking over into this science. In his time one could have discarded the old way of inquiry, retained the mystical disposition, and accepted modern natural science, had it already existed.

But what the human soul finds compatible with a way of inquiry it must, if it is strong enough, also be able to extract from it.

I wanted to describe the characteristics of medieval mysticism in order to indicate how, separated from its native soil, the old way of conceiving things, it develops into an independent mysticism, but cannot preserve itself because it now lacks the spiritual impulse which, through its connection with inquiry, it had in earlier times.

This leads to the thought that those elements of more recent research which lead to mysticism must be sought for. From this inquiry the spiritual impulse which does not stop at the darkly mystical, emotional inner life, but ascends from the mystical starting-point to a knowledge of the spirits, can be regained. Medieval mysticism atrophied because it had lost the substratum of inquiry which directs the faculties of the soul upward to the spirit. This book is intended to provide a stimulus for extracting from more recent inquiry, when properly understood, those forces which are directed toward the spiritual world.

Goetheanum in Dornach bei Basel, Switzerland
Autumn 1923

RUDOLF STEINER

MYSTICISM
AT THE DAWN OF THE MODERN AGE

INTRODUCTION

THERE ARE MAGIC formulas which continue to act in perpetually new ways throughout the centuries of the history of ideas. In Greece one such formula was regarded as an oracle of Apollo. It is, "Know thyself." Such sentences seem to contain an infinite life within themselves. One meets them in walking the most diverse paths of spiritual life. The more one advances, the more one penetrates to an understanding of all phenomena, the deeper appears the meaning of these formulas. At many moments in the course of our meditations and thoughts they flash like lightning, illuminating our whole inner life. At such times there arises in us something like the feeling that we perceive the heartbeat of humanity's development. How close we feel to personalities of the past when one of their sayings arouses in us the sensation that they are revealing to us the fact of their having had such moments! One then feels oneself brought into an intimate relationship with these personalities. Thus for instance, one becomes intimately acquainted with Hegel when, in the third volume of his *Vorlesungen über die Geschichte der*

Philosophie, Lectures on the History of Philosophy, one
comes upon the words: "Such stuff, one says, are the abstractions we behold when we let the philosophers
dispute and quarrel in our study, and decide matters in
this way or in that; these are abstractions made up of
mere words.—No! No! They are acts of the universal spirit,
and therefore of fate. In this the philosophers are closer
to the master than those who feed upon the crumbs of
the spirit; they read or write the cabinet orders in the
original: it is their function to take part in writing them.
The philosophers are the mystics who were present at
the act in the innermost sanctuary and who participated
in it." When Hegel said this he experienced one of the
moments described above. He spoke these sentences when
he had reached the end of Greek philosophy in the course
of his analysis. And through them he has shown that the
meaning of Neoplatonist wisdom, of which he speaks at
this point, was at one time illuminated for him as by a
stroke of lightning. At the moment of this illumination
he had become intimate with such spirits as Plotinus and
Proclus. And we become intimate with him as we read
his words.

And we become intimate with the solitarily meditating
vicar in Zschopau, M. Valentinus Wigelius (Valentin
Weigel), when we read the words of introduction to his
booklet, *Erkenne dich selbst,* Know Thyself, written in
1578. "We read in the old sages the useful proverb, 'Know
thyself,' which, although it is principally used to refer to
worldly behavior, such as, Look well at yourself, what you
are; Search in your bosom; Judge yourself, and leave

others uncensored: although it is, I say, used in human life with respect to behavior, yet we may well apply this saying, 'Know thyself,' to the natural and supernatural understanding of the whole man, so that man shall not only look at himself and thus remember what his behavior should be with respect to other people, but also understand his nature, internally and externally, in the spirit and in nature: whence he comes, of what he is made, and what he is meant for." From his own points of view Valentin Weigel has thus arrived at insights which were summed up for him in the oracle of Apollo.

A similar road to understanding, and the same position with respect to the "Know thyself," can be ascribed to a series of penetrating spirits beginning with Meister Eckhart (1260-1327) and ending with Angelus Silesius (1624-1677), to which Valentin Weigel also belongs.

What is common to these spirits is a strong feeling that in man's self-knowledge arises a sun which illuminates something beyond the incidental individual personality of the beholder. What Spinoza realized in the ethereal height of pure thought, that "the human soul has a sufficient knowledge of the eternal and infinite nature of God," lived in them as immediate perception; and for them self-knowledge was the path by which this eternal and infinite nature was to be reached. It was clear to them that self-knowledge in its true form endows man with a new sense which opens to him a world that has the same relation to what can be attained without this sense as does the world of the physically sighted to that of the blind. It would not be easy to find a better description of the importance of this new sense than that given by J. G. Fichte in his Berlin lectures in the year 1813. "Imagine a world of people born blind, who therefore know only those objects and their conditions which exist through the sense of touch. Go among them and speak to them of colors and of the other conditions which exist only for sight through the medium of light. Either you will speak to them of nothing, and it will be better if they say so, for in this way you will soon notice your mistake, and, if you cannot open their eyes, will put an end to this fruitless talk.—Or for some reason they will want to give a meaning to your teaching; in this case they will only be able to understand it through what they know from touch: they will want to feel the light, the colors, and the other conditions of visibility; they will think that they feel them, will, within the realm of touch, make up something that they call color and deceive themselves with it. Then they will misunderstand, turn things around, and misinterpret." Something similar may be said of that toward which the spirits under discussion strove. In self-knowledge they saw the opening up of a new sense. And in their opinion this sense leads to insights which do not exist for one who does not perceive in self-knowledge that which differentiates it from all other kinds of knowing. One to whom this sense has not opened itself thinks that self-knowledge arises in a way similar to knowledge through external senses, or through some other means acting from the outside. He thinks, "Knowledge is knowledge." However, in one case its object is something situated in the external world, in the other case it is in his own soul. He hears only words, at best abstract thoughts, in what, for those who look deeper, constitutes the basis of their inner life: namely, in the dictum that in all other kinds of knowing the object is outside of ourselves, while in self-knowledge we stand inside the object; that every other object comes into contact with us as something completed and closed, while in our self we actively and creatively weave what we observe in ourselves. This may appear as an explanation consisting of mere words, perhaps as a triviality, but if properly understood, it can also appear as a higher light which illuminates all other knowledge in a new way. He to whom it appears under the first aspect is in the same situation as a blind man to whom one says, A brilliant object is there. He hears the words, but for him brilliance does not exist. One can unite in oneself the sum of the knowledge of a period; if one does not perceive the significance of self-knowledge then in the higher sense all knowledge is but blind.

Independent of us, the world lives for us because it communicates itself to our spirit. What is communicated to us must be expressed in the language characteristic of us. A book would be meaningless for us if its contents were to be presented to us in an unknown tongue. In the same way the world would be meaningless for us if it did not speak to us in our language. The same language which reaches us from the realm of objects, we also hear in ourselves. But then it *is* we who are speaking. It is only a matter of listening aright to the transformation which occurs when we close our perception to external

objects and listen only to that which then sounds in ourselves. It is for this that the new sense is necessary. If it is
not awakened we think that in the communications about
ourselves we perceive only communications about an object external to ourselves; we are of the opinion that there
is something hidden somewhere which speaks to us in the
same way as do external objects. If we have the new sense
we know that its perceptions are quite different from those
which refer to external objects. Then we know that this
sense does not leave outside of itself that which it perceives, as the eye leaves outside of itself the object it sees,
but that it can completely incorporate its object within
itself. If I see an object, the object remains outside of me;
if I perceive myself, I myself enter into my perception.
One who seeks some part of his self outside what is perceived, shows that the essential content of what is perceived has not become apparent to him. Johannes Tauler
(1300-1361) expressed this truth in the apt words: If I
were a king and did not know it, I would not be a king.
If I do not become clear to myself in my self-perception,
then I do not exist for myself. But if I do become clear
to myself then in my most fundamental nature I *possess*
myself in my perception. No part of me remains outside
of my perception. J. G. Fichte strongly indicates the difference between self-perception and every other kind of
perception in the following words: "It would be easier
to get most people to consider themselves to be a piece
of lava in the moon than a *self*. He who is not in agreement with himself about this understands no thorough-
going philosophy and needs none. Nature, whose machine

he is, will lead him without his doing anything in all the acts he has to perform. In order to philosophize one needs independence, and this one can only give to oneself.—We should not want to see without eyes, but we should also not affirm that it is the eye which sees."

The perception of oneself is thus at the same time an *awakening* of the self. In our knowing we connect the nature of things with our own nature. The communications which things make to us in our language become parts of our own self. A thing which confronts me is no longer separate from me once I know it. That part of it which I can take in is incorporated into my own nature. When I awaken my own self, when I perceive what is within me, then I also awaken to a higher existence what I have incorporated into my nature from the outside. The light which falls upon me when I awaken, also falls upon what I have appropriated to myself of the things of the world. A light flashes in me and illuminates me, and with me everything I know of the world. Everything I know would remain blind knowledge if this light did not fall upon it. I could penetrate the whole world with my knowledge; it would not be what it must become in me if knowledge were not awakened to a higher existence within me.

What I add to things by this awakening is not a new idea, is not an enrichment of the content of my knowledge; it is a raising of knowledge, of cognition, to a higher level, on which everything is endowed with a new brilliance. As long as I do not raise my cognition to this level, all knowledge remains worthless to me in the higher sense. Things exist without me too. They have their being in themselves. What does it mean if with their existence, which they have outside without me, I connect another spiritual existence, which repeats things within me? If it were a matter of a mere repetition of things, it would be senseless to do this.—But it is a matter of a mere repetition only so long as I do not awaken to a higher existence within my own self the spiritual content of things received into myself. When this happens, then I have not repeated the nature of things within me, but have given it a re-birth on a higher level. With the awakening of my self there takes place a spiritual *rebirth* of the things of the world. What things show in this rebirth they did not possess previously. There outside stands a tree. I take it into my mind. I throw my inner light upon what I have apprehended. Within me the tree becomes more than it is outside. That part of it which enters through the portal of the senses is received into a spiritual content. An ideal counterpart to the tree is in me. This says infinitely much about the tree, which the tree outside cannot tell me. *What* the tree is only shines upon it out of me. Now the tree is no longer the isolated being which it is in external space. It becomes a part of the whole spiritual world living within me. It combines its content with other ideas which exist in me. It becomes a part of the whole world of ideas, which embraces the vegetable kingdom; it is further integrated into the evolutionary scale of every living thing.—Another example: I throw a stone in a horizontal direction. It moves in a curved line, and after some time falls to the ground. In successive moments of time I see it in different locations. Through reflection I arrive at the following: During its movement the stone is subject to differing influences. If it were only under the influence of the impulse I gave to it, it would fly on forever in a straight line, without any change in its velocity. But the earth also exercises an influence upon it. It attracts it. If I had simply let it go without giving it an impulse, it would have fallen vertically to the earth. During the fall its velocity would have constantly increased. The reciprocal action of these two influences produces what I actually see.—Let us assume that I was not able to separate the two influences mentally, and to reconstruct mentally what I see from their combination according to certain laws; matters would remain at that which is seen. It would be a spiritually blind looking-on, a perception of the successive positions occupied by the stone. But in fact matters do *not* remain at this. The whole process occurs twice. Once outside, and there my eye sees it; then my mind lets the whole process occur again, in a mental fashion. My inner sense must be directed upon the mental process, which my eye does not see, in order for it to realize that with my own forces I awaken the process in its mental aspect.—One can again adduce a dictum of J. G. Fichte, which makes this fact clearly intelligible. "The new sense is thus the sense for the spirit; that sense for which *only* the spirit exists and nothing else, and for which the other, the given existence, also assumes the form of the spirit and becomes transformed into it, for which therefore existence in its own form has actually disappeared. . . . This sense has been used for seeing as long as men have existed, and everything great and excellent in the world, and which alone makes mankind endure, has its origin in the visions of this sense. But it was not the case that this sense saw itself in its difference from and its opposition to the other, ordinary sense. The impressions of the two senses became fused; life split into these two halves without a unifying bond." The unifying bond is created by the fact that the inner sense perceives the spiritual, which it awakens in its intercourse with the external world, in its spirituality. Because of this, that part of things which we take up into our spirit ceases to appear as a meaningless repetition. It appears as something new in opposition to what external perception can give. The simple process of throwing a stone, and my perception of it, appear in a higher light when I make clear to myself the task of my inner sense in this whole matter. In order to combine intellectually the two influences and their manners of acting, a sum of mental content is required which I must already have acquired when I perceive the flying stone. I thus *use* a mental content already stored within me upon something which confronts me in the external world. And this process of the external world is integrated into the pre-existing intellectual content. In its essence it shows itself to be an expression of this content. Through a comprehension of my inner sense the relationship of the content of this sense to the things of the external world thus becomes apparent to me. Fichte could say that without a comprehension of this sense, for me the world splits into two halves: into things outside of me, and into images of these things within me. The two halves become united when the inner sense understands *itself,* and therewith realizes what kind of light it sheds upon things in the process of cognition. And Fichte could also say that this inner sense sees *only* spirit. For it sees how the spirit illuminates the world of the senses by integrating it into the world of the spiritual. The inner sense lets the external sensory existence arise within it as a spiritual essence on a higher level. An external thing is completely known when there is no part of it which has not experienced a spiritual rebirth in this way. Every external thing is thus integrated with a spiritual content, which, when it is seized upon by the inner sense, participates in the destiny of self-knowledge. The spiritual content which belongs to a thing enters wholly into the world of ideas through the illumination from inside, just as does our own self.—This exposition contains nothing which is either capable of a *logical* proof or requires one. It is nothing but a result of inner experiences. One who denies its purport only shows that he lacks this inner experience. One cannot dispute with him any more than one disputes about color with a blind man.—It must not however be asserted that this inner experience is made possible only through the gift possessed by a few chosen ones. It is a common human quality. Everyone who does not refuse to do so can enter upon the path to it. This refusal however is frequent enough. And one always has the feeling when one meets with objections made in this vein: it is not a matter of people who cannot acquire the inner experience, but of those who block their access to it by a net of various logical chimeras. It is almost as if someone who looks through a telescope sees a new planet, but nevertheless denies its existence because his *calculations* have shown him that there can be no planet in that location.

At the same time there exists in most people a definite feeling that with what the external senses and the analytic intellect perceive, not all of the nature of things can be given. They then think that the remainder must lie in the outside world, just as do the objects of external perception themselves. What they should attain by perceiving again, with the inner sense and on a higher level, that is, the object which they have perceived and seized upon with the intellect, they displace into the outside world as something inaccessible and unknown. They then speak of limits to cognition which prevent us from attaining the "thing in itself." They speak of the unknown "nature" of things. That this "nature" of things becomes clear when the inner sense lets its light fall upon things, they will not acknowledge. An especially telling example of the error which lies hidden here was furnished by the famous "Ignorabimus" speech of the scientist, Du Bois-Reymond, in the year 1876. Everywhere we should go only so far as to see manifestations of "matter" in the processes of nature. Of what "matter" itself is, we are not to know anything. Du Bois-Reymond asserts that we shall never be able to penetrate to the point where matter haunts space. But the reason we cannot penetrate to this point lies in the fact that nothing whatsoever can be found there. One who speaks like Du Bois-Reymond has a feeling that the understanding of nature gives results which point to something else, which this understanding itself cannot give. But he does not want to enter upon the path which leads to this something else, namely the path of inner experience. Therefore he is helpless when confronted by the question of "matter," as by a dark mystery. In the one who enters upon the path of inner experience things come to a rebirth; and what in them remains unknown to external experience then becomes clear.

Thus the inner life of man not only elucidates itself, but also external things. From this point an infinite perspective for human cognition opens up. Within glows a light which does not confine its luminosity to this interior. It is a sun which illuminates *all* reality at once. Something appears in us which unites us with the whole world. We are no longer merely the single accidental man, no longer this or that individual. In us the whole world reveals itself. To us it discloses its own interconnection, and it shows us how we ourselves as individuals are connected with it. Out of self-knowledge is born knowledge of the world. And our own limited individuality takes its place spiritually in the great interconnection of the world because something comes to life in it which reaches beyond this individuality, which embraces everything of which this individuality is a part.

Thinking which with logical prejudices does not block its way to inner experience will at last always reach a recognition of the essential nature working within us, which connects us with the whole world, because through it we overcome the contrast of inner and outer where man is concerned. Paul Asmus, the prematurely deceased, clear-sighted philosopher, comments on this state of affairs in the following way (cf. his work: *Das Ich und das Ding an sich,* The Self and the Thing in Itself, p. 14f.): "We shall make this clearer to ourselves by means of an example. Let us imagine a piece of sugar; it is round, sweet, impenetrable, etc.; all these are qualities we understand; there is only one thing in all this that appears to us as something absolutely different, that we do not understand, that is so different from us that we cannot penetrate into it without losing ourselves, from the mere surface of which our thought timidly recoils. This one thing is the bearer of all these qualities, and is unknown to us; it is the very essence which constitutes the innermost self of this object. Thus Hegel says correctly that the whole content of our idea is only related to this dark subject as an accident, and that we only attach qualifications to this essence without penetrating to its depths,—qualifications which finally, since we do not know it itself, have no truly objective value, are subjective. Comprehending thinking, on the other hand, has no such unknowable subject in which its qualifications are only accidents, *rather the objective subject falls within the concept.* If I comprehend something, it is present in my concept in its totality; I am at home in the innermost sanctuary of its nature, not because it has no essence of its own, but because it compels me, *through the necessity, poised over both of us,* of the concept, which appears subjectively in me, objectively in it, to *re*-think its concept. Through this *re*-thinking there is revealed to us, as Hegel says,—just as this is our subjective activity,—*at the same time the true nature of the object.*"—Only he can speak in this way who is able to illuminate the processes of thought with the light of inner experience.

In my *Philosophie der Freiheit,* Philosophy of Spiritual Activity, departing from different points of view, I also have pointed to the primordial fact of the inner life: "There is thus no doubt: in thinking we hold the universal processes by a corner where we have to be present if they are to take place at all. And it is just this which is important. This is just the reason why things confront me in such a mysterious fashion, that I am so unconcerned with the process of their becoming. I simply come upon them, but in thinking I know how it is done. Therefore there is no more primordial point of departure for the contemplation of the universal processes than thinking."

To the one who regards the inner experience of man in this way the meaning of human cognition within the whole universal process is also clear. It is not an unimportant addition to the rest of the universal process. This is what it would be if it represented only a repetition, in the form of ideas, of what exists externally. But in *understanding* occurs what does not occur anywhere in the external world: the universal process confronts itself with its own spiritual nature. This universal process would be forever incomplete if this confrontation did not take place. With it the inner experience of man becomes integrated into the objective universal process; the latter would be incomplete without it.

It can be seen that only that life which is dominated by the inner sense, man's highest spiritual life in the truest sense, thus raises him above himself. For it is only in this life that the nature of things is revealed in confrontation with itself. Matters are different with the lower faculty of perception. The eye for instance, which mediates the sight of an object, is the scene of a process which, in relation to the inner life, is completely similar to any other external process. My organs are parts of the spatial world like other things, and their perceptions are temporal processes like others. Their nature too only becomes apparent when they are submerged in the inner experience. I thus live a double life: the life of a thing among other things, which lives within its corporeality and through its organs perceives what lies outside this corporeality, and above this life a higher one, which knows no such inside and outside, and extends over both the external world and itself. I shall therefore have to say: At one time I am an individual, a limited I; at the other time I am a general, universal I. This too Paul Asmus has put into apt words (cf. his book: *Die indogermanischen Religionen in den Hauptpunkten ihrer Entwicklung,* The Indo-European Religions in the Main Points of their Development, p. 29 of the first volume): "We call the activity of submerging ourselves in something else, 'thinking;' in thinking the I has fulfilled its concept, it has given up its existence as something separate; therefore in thinking we find ourselves in a sphere that is the same for all, for the principle of isolation, which lies in the relationship of our I to what is different from it, has disappeared in the activity of the self-suspension of the separate I; there is only *the selfhood common to all.*"

Spinoza has exactly the same thing in mind when he describes the highest activity of cognition as that which advances "from the sufficient conception of the real nature of some attributes of God to the sufficient cognition of the nature of things." This advance is nothing other than illumination of things with the light of inner experience. Spinoza describes the life of this inner experience in glorious colors: "The highest virtue of the soul is to apprehend God, or to comprehend things in the third—the highest—kind of cognition. This virtue becomes the greater the more the soul comprehends things in this way of cognition; therefore the one who grasps things in this way of cognition attains the highest human perfection and consequently becomes filled with the highest joy, accompanied by the conceptions of himself and of virtue. Hence from this kind of cognition springs the highest possible peace of soul." One who comprehends things in this way transforms himself within himself; for at such moments his separate I is absorbed by the All-I; all beings do not appear in subordination to a separate, limited individual; they appear to themselves. At this level there is no longer any difference between Plato and me; what separates us belongs to a lower level of cognition. We are only separate as individuals; the universal which acts in us is one and the same. About this fact also one cannot dispute with one who has no experience of it. He will always insist: Plato and you are two. That this duality, that all multiplicity is reborn as unity in the unfolding of the highest level of cognition, cannot be proved: it must be *experienced*. Paradoxical as it may sound, it is true: the idea which Plato represented to himself and the same idea which I represent to myself are not two ideas. They are one and the same idea. And there are not two ideas, one in Plato's head, the other in mine; rather in the higher sense Plato's head and mine interpenetrate; all heads which grasp the same, *single* idea, interpenetrate; and this unique idea exists only once. It is there, and the heads all transport themselves to one and the same place in order to contain this idea.

The transformation which is effected in the whole nature of man when he looks at things in this way is indicated in beautiful words in the Indian poem, *The Bhagavad Gita,* of which Wilhelm von Humboldt therefore said that he was grateful to his destiny for having permitted him to live until he could be in a position to become acquainted with this work. The inner light says in this poem, "An external ray from me, who has attained to a special existence in the world of personal life, attracts to itself the five senses and the individual soul, which belong to nature.—When the effulgent spirit materializes in space and time, or when it dematerializes, it seizes upon things and carries them along with itself, as the breath of the wind seizes upon the perfumes of flowers and sweeps them away with itself.—The inner light dominates the ear, the touch, the taste, and the smell, as well as the mind; it forms a bond between itself and the things of the senses.—Fools do not know when the inner light flames up and when it is extinguished, or when it unites with things; only he who partakes of the inner light can know of this." So strongly does *The Bhagavad Gita* point to the transformation of man that it says of the "sage" that he can no longer err, no longer sin. If he seems to err or sin he must illuminate his thoughts or his actions with a light in which that no longer appears as error and as sin which appears as such to the ordinary consciousness. "He who has raised himself and whose knowledge is of the purest kind does not kill and does not defile himself, even though he should slay another." This only indicates the same basic disposition of the soul, springing from the highest cognition, concerning which Spinoza, after describing it in his *Ethics,* breaks into the thrilling words: "With this I have concluded what I wanted to set forth concerning the power of the soul over the affections and over the freedom of the soul. From this it appears how superior is a wise man to an ignorant one, and how much more powerful than one who is merely driven by passions. For the ignorant man is not only driven in many directions by external causes and never attains to true peace of soul, but he also lives in ignorance of himself, of God, and of objects, and when his suffering comes to an end, his existence also comes to an end; while the wise man, as such, hardly experiences any agitation in his spirit, but rather never ceases to exist in the as it were necessary knowledge of himself, of God, and of objects, and always enjoys true peace of soul. Although the path I have described as leading to this appears very difficult, it can be found nevertheless. And it may well be troublesome, since it is found so seldom. For how is it possible that, if salvation were close at hand and to be found without great effort, it is neglected by almost everyone? But everything sublime is as difficult as it is rare."

Goethe has adumbrated the point of view of the highest

cognition in monumental fashion in the words: "If I know my relationship to myself and to the external world, I call it truth. And thus everyone can have his own truth, and it is still always the same truth." Everyone has his own truth, because everyone is an individual, distinct being beside and together with others. These other beings act upon him through his organs. From the individual point of view, where he is placed, and according to the nature of his faculty of perception, he forms his own truth in intercourse with things. He achieves his relationship to things. Then when he enters into self-knowledge, when he comes to know his relationship to himself, his particular truth becomes dissolved in the general truth; this general truth is the same in everyone.

The understanding of the suspension of what is individual in the personality, of the I in favor of the all-I, is regarded by deeper natures as the secret revealing itself within man, as the primordial mystery of life. For this too Goethe has found an apt expression: "And as long as you do not have it, this Die and Become, you are only a dreary guest on the dark earth."

What takes place in the inner life of man is not a mental repetition, but a real part of the universal process. The world would not be what it is if it were not active in the human soul. And if one calls the highest which is attainable by man the divine, then one must say that the divine does not exist as something external to be repeated as an *image* in the human spirit, but that the divine is *awakened* in man. For this Angelus Silesius has found the right words: "I know that *without me* God cannot live for a moment; if I come to naught He must needs give up the ghost." "God cannot make a single worm without me; if I do not preserve it with Him, it must fall apart forthwith." Such an assertion can only be made by one who premises that something appears in man without which an external being cannot exist. If everything which belongs to the "worm" also existed without man, it would be impossible to say that the worm must "fall apart" if man does not preserve it.

In self-knowledge the innermost core of the world comes to life as spiritual content. For man, the experiencing of self-knowledge means an acting within the core of the world. One who is penetrated by self-knowledge naturally also performs his own actions in the light of self-knowledge. In general, human action is determined by *motives*. Robert Hamerling, the poet-philosopher, has rightly said (*Atomistik des Willens*, Atomism of the Will, p. 213f.): "It is true that man can do what he wills, but he cannot will what he wills, because his will is determined by *motives.*—He cannot will what he wills. Let us examine these words more closely. Do they contain a rational meaning? Would freedom of willing then consist in being able to will something without cause, without motive? But what does willing mean if not *to have a cause* for preferring to do or to aspire to this rather than that? To will something without cause, without motive, would mean to will something *without willing it*. The concept of motive is inseparably connected with that of willing. Without a definite motive the will is an empty *capacity;* only through the motive does it become active and real. It is thus quite correct that the human will is not free insofar as its direction is always determined by the strongest motive." For every action which does not take place in the light of self-knowledge the motive, the cause of the action must be felt as a compulsion. Matters are different when the cause is included within the bounds of self-knowledge. Then this cause has become a part of the self. The will is no longer determined; it determines itself. The conformity to laws, the motives of willing, now no longer predominate *over* the one who wills; they are one and the same with this willing. To illuminate one's actions with the light of self-observation means to overcome all coercion by motives. Thereby the will places itself into the realm of *freedom*.

Not all human actions bear the character of freedom. Only that acting which is inspired in each one of its parts by self-observation is free. And because self-observation raises the individual I to the general I, free acting is that which proceeds from the all-I. The old issue of whether the will of man is free or subordinated to a general regularity, an unalterable necessity, is an improperly posed question. Those actions which are performed by man as an individual are unfree; those are free which he performs after his spiritual rebirth. Man is thus, in general, not *either* free *or* unfree. He is the *one* as well as the *other*. He is unfree before his rebirth, and he can *become* free through this rebirth. The individual upward development of man consists in the *transformation* of this unfree willing into one which bears the character of freedom. The man who has penetrated the regularity of his actions as being his own, has overcome the compulsion of this regularity, and therewith his unfreedom. Freedom is not a fact of human existence *from the first,* but rather a *goal.*

With free acting man resolves a contradiction between the world and himself. His own deeds become deeds of the universal existence. He feels himself to be in full harmony with this universal existence. Each dissonance between himself and another he feels to be the result of a not yet fully awakened self. But the destiny of the self is that only in its separation from the universe can it find contact with this universe. Man would not be man if as an I he were not separated from everything else; but he would not be man in the highest sense if, as such a separated I, he did not enlarge himself out of himself to the all-I. Above all, it is characteristic of human nature that it should overcome a contradiction which originally lies within it.

The one who will allow spirit to be only the logical intellect may feel his blood run cold at the thought that things should experience their rebirth in the spirit. He will compare the fresh, living flower outside, in the fullness of its colors, with the cold, pale, schematic *thought* of the flower. He will feel especially uncomfortable at the idea that the man who takes his motives for acting out of the solitude of his self-knowledge should be freer than the spontaneous, naïve personality which acts out of its immediate impulses, out of the fullness of its nature. To such a man, who sees only the one-sided logical aspect, one who submerges himself within himself will appear as a walking schema of concepts, as a phantom, in contrast to one who remains in his natural individuality.—One

hears such objections to the rebirth of things in the spirit
especially among those who are, it is true, equipped with
healthy organs for sensory perception and with lively
drives and passions, but whose faculty of observation fails
when confronted with objects of a purely spiritual content. As soon as they are expected to perceive something
purely spiritual, their perception is wanting; they are
dealing with the mere shells of concepts, if not indeed
with empty words. Therefore, when it is a matter of
spiritual content, they remain the "dry," "abstract men
of intellect." But for one who has a gift of observation
in the purely spiritual like that in the sensory realm, life
naturally does not become poorer when he enriches it
with spiritual content. I look at a flower; why should its
rich colors lose even the smallest part of their freshness
if it is not only my eye which sees the colors, but *also*
my inner sense which sees the spiritual nature of the
flower as well. Why should the life of my personality become poorer if I do not follow my passions and impulses
in spiritual blindness, but rather irradiate them with the
light of a higher knowledge. Not poorer, but fuller, richer
is the life reflected in spirit.[1]

---

[1] See Addendum I.

MEISTER ECKHART

WHOLLY IRRADIATED by the feeling that things are reborn as higher entities in the spirit of man, is the conceptual world of Meister Eckhart. He belonged to the Order of the Dominicans, as did the greatest Christian theologian of the Middle Ages, Thomas Aquinas, who lived from 1225 to 1274. Eckhart was an admirer of Thomas in the fullest sense. This is altogether understandable when one examines the whole conceptual framework of Meister Eckhart. He considered himself to be as much in harmony with the teachings of the Christian church as he assumed such an agreement for Thomas. Eckhart did not want to take anything away from the content of Christianity, nor to add anything to it. But he wanted to produce this content anew in *his* way. It is not among the spiritual needs of a personality such as he was to put new truths of various kinds in place of old ones. He was intimately connected with the content which had been transmitted to him. But he wanted to give a new form, a new life to this content. Without doubt he wanted to remain an orthodox Christian. The Christian truths were his truths. Only he wanted to look at them in a different way than had Thomas Aquinas, for instance. The latter assumed two sources of knowledge: *revelation* for faith, and *reason* for inquiry. Reason understands the laws of things, that is, the spiritual in nature. It can also raise itself above nature, and in the spirit grasp, from one side, the divine essence which underlies all nature. But in this way it does not achieve an immersion in the *full* essence of God. A higher truth must meet it halfway. This is given in the Scriptures. It *reveals* what by himself man cannot attain. The truth of the Scriptures must be taken for granted by man; reason can defend it, can endeavor to understand it as well as possible by means of its powers of cognition, but it can never produce it out of the human spirit. What the spirit *sees* is not the *highest* truth, but is a certain cognitive content which has come to the spirit *from outside*. St. Augustine declares that within himself he is unable to find the source of what he *should believe*. He says, "I would not believe the Gospel if the authority of the Catholic church did not move me to do so." This is in the sense of the Evangelist, who refers us to the external testimony: "That which we have heard, which we have seen with our eyes, which we have looked upon, and our hands have handled, of the Word of life . . . . that which we have seen and heard declare we unto you, that ye also may have fellowship with us." But Meister Eckhart wishes to impress upon men Christ's words: "It is expedient for you that I go away: for if I go not away, the Comforter [in the German version, *der heilige Geist,* i.e., the Holy Ghost] will not come unto you." And he explains these words by saying, "It is as if he said: You have taken too much joy in my *present image,* therefore the perfect joy of the Holy Ghost cannot be in you." Eckhart thinks that he is speaking of no God other than the one of whom Augustine and the Evangelist and Thomas speak, and yet their testimony of God is not his testimony. "Some people want to look upon God with their eyes, as they look upon a cow, and want to love God as they love a cow. Thus they love God for the sake of external riches and of internal solace; but these people do not love God aright. . . . Foolish people deem that they should look upon God as though He stood there and they here. It is not thus. God and I are one in the act of knowing." Such declarations in Eckhart are based on nothing but the experience of the inner sense. And this experience shows things to him in a higher light. He therefore does not think that he needs an external light in order to attain to the highest insights: "A master says, God has become man; through this all mankind is raised and exalted. Let us rejoice that Christ our brother has ascended by his own strength above all the angelic choirs and sits on the right hand of the Father. This master has spoken well, but in truth, I do not set great store by it. What would it avail me if I had a brother who was a rich man, and for my part I were a poor man? What would it avail me if I had a brother who was a wise man, and I were a fool? . . . The Heavenly Father brings forth his only-begotten Son in Himself and *in me*. Why in Himself and in me? I am one with Him, and He cannot shut me out. In the same act the Holy Ghost receives its being, and it arises through me as it does through God. Why? I am in God, and if the

Holy Ghost does not take its being from me it does not take it from God either. I am not shut out in any way." When Eckhart reminds us of the word of Paul: "Clothe yourselves in Jesus Christ," he wishes to give to this word the following meaning: Become submerged in yourselves, plunge down into self-contemplation, and from the depths of your being God will shine upon you; He will outshine everything for you; you have found Him within your-selves; you have become united with God's essence. "God has become man so that I might become God." In his treatise *Über die Abgeschiedenheit,* Concerning Solitude, Eckhart expresses himself on the relationship of external to internal perception: "Here you must know that the masters say that in each man there are two kinds of men: one is called the external man, that is, sensuousness; man is served by five senses, nevertheless he acts through the force of the soul. The other man is called the inner man, that is, the interior of man. Now you must know that every man who loves God does not use the faculties of the soul in the external man any more than is required by the five senses; and the interior does not turn to the five senses except as it is the director and guide of the five senses and watches over them so that, in their strivings, they do not pander to animality." One who speaks in this way about the inner man can no longer fix his eye upon a *nature* of things which lies sensorily *outside him.* For he is aware that this *nature* cannot confront him in any kind of sen-sory outside world. To him one might object, What have the things in the outside world to do with what you add to them out of your spirit. Trust your senses. They alone

give you intelligence of the outside world. Do not falsify
with a spiritual trimming what your senses give you in
purity, without decoration, as a picture of the external
world. Your eye tells you what a color is like; nothing
that your spirit apprehends concerning the color is in the
color. From the point of view of Meister Eckhart one
would have to answer: the senses are physical devices.
Their communications about things therefore can concern
only the physical aspect of things. And this physical aspect of things communicates itself to me by the excitation
of a physical process within myself. Color as a physical
process of the outside world gives rise to a physical process
in my eye and in my brain. Through this I perceive the
color. But in this way I can perceive in the color only
what is physical, sensory. Sensory perception excludes all
those aspects of things which are not sensory. It divests
things of all that is not sensory in them. If I then proceed
to the spiritual, the idea-content, I only re-establish that
aspect of things which sensory perception has effaced.
Hence sensory perception does not show me the deepest
nature of things; rather it separates me from this nature.
Spiritual comprehension, comprehension by the idea,
again connects me with this nature. It shows me that
within themselves things are of exactly the same spiritual
nature as I myself. The boundary between me and the external world is abolished by the spiritual comprehension
of the world. I am separated from the external world insofar as I am a sensory thing among sensory things. My
eye and the color are two different entities. My brain and
the plant are two. But the idea-content of the plant and

of the color, together with the idea-content of my brain and of the eye, belong to a unified idea-entity.—This view must not be confused with the widespread anthropomorphizing world view which thinks that it comprehends the things of the external world by ascribing to them qualities of a psychical nature, which are supposed to be similar to the qualities of the human soul. This view says: When he confronts us externally, we perceive only sensory features in another man. I cannot look into the interior of my fellow man. From what I see and hear of him I make inferences as to his interior, his soul. Thus the soul is never something I perceive directly. A soul I perceive only within myself. No man sees my thoughts, my imaginings, my feelings. And just as *I* have such an inner life beside the one which can be perceived externally, so all other beings must have one too. This is the conclusion of one who takes the position of the anthropomorphizing world view. That part of a plant which I perceive externally must in the same way be only the outside of an interior, of a soul, which in my thoughts I must add to what I perceive. And since there exists for me only a single inner world, namely my own, I can only imagine the inner world of other beings to be similar to my own. Thus one reaches a sort of universal animation of all nature (panpsychism). This view rests on a misunderstanding of what the developed inner sense really offers. The spiritual content of an external thing, which appears to me within myself, is not something added in thought to the external perception. It is no more this than is the spirit of another man. I perceive this spiritual content through the inner sense, just as I perceive the physical content through the external senses. And what I call my inner life, in the sense indicated above, is by no means my spirit in the higher sense. This inner life is only the result of purely sensory processes; it belongs to me only as a totally individual personality, which is nothing but the result of its physical organization. When I transfer this interior to external things, I am in fact indulging in idle fancy. My personal inner life, my thoughts, memories, and feelings are in me because I am a creature of nature with such and such an organization, with a certain sensory apparatus, with a certain nervous system. I cannot transfer this *human* soul of mine to things. I could do this only if somewhere I found a similarly organized nervous system. But my individual soul is not the highest spiritual part in me. This highest spiritual part must first be awakened in me by the inner sense. And this spiritual part which is awakened in me is at the same time one and the same with the spiritual in all things. Before this spiritual part the plant appears directly in its own spirituality. I need not endow it with a spirituality similar to my own. For *this* world view all talk about the unknown "thing in itself" becomes devoid of meaning. For it is precisely the "thing in itself" which reveals itself to the inner sense. All talk about the unknown "thing in itself" is only due to the fact that those who speak in this way are incapable of recognizing the "things in themselves" in the spiritual contents within them. They think that within themselves they recognize only unsubstantial shadows and phantoms, "mere concepts and ideas" of things. But nevertheless since they have an *intimation* of the "thing in itself" they think that this "thing in itself" conceals itself, and that limits are set to the human powers of cognition. One cannot prove to those who labor under this belief that they must seize the "thing in itself" within themselves, for they never would acknowledge this "thing in itself" if one showed it to them. And it is just a matter of this *acknowledgment*.— Everything Meister Eckhart says is penetrated by this acknowledgment. "Consider a simile for this. A door opens and closes on a hinge. If I compare the outer boards of the door to the external man, then I shall compare the hinge to the inner man. Now when the door opens and closes the outer boards move back and forth, while the hinge remains constantly immobile, and in no way is changed thereby. And here it is the same." As an individual creature of the senses I can investigate things in all directions—the door opens and closes—; if I do not let the perceptions of the senses arise within me spiritually I shall know nothing of their essence—the hinge does not move—. The illumination mediated by the inner sense is, in Eckhart's conception, the entry of God into the soul. He calls the light of knowledge which is lit by this entry, the "spark of the soul." The place within the human being where this "spark" is lighted is "so pure, and so high, and so noble in itself, that no creature can be in it, but only God alone dwells therein in His pure divine nature." One who has let this "spark" light up within himself, no longer sees *merely* as man sees with the external senses, and with the logical intellect, which orders and classifies the impressions of the senses; rather he sees how things are in themselves. The external senses and the ordering intellect separate the individual human being from other things; they make of him an individual in space and in time, who also perceives other things in space and in time. The man illuminated by the "spark" ceases to be an individual being. He annihilates his isolation. Everything which causes the difference between him and things, ceases. That it is *he* as an individual being who perceives, no longer can even be taken into consideration. The things and he are no longer separated. The things, and thus also God, see themselves in him. "This spark is God, in such a way that it is an united one, and carries within itself the image of all creatures, image without image, and image above image." In the most magnificent words does Eckhart speak of the extinction of the individual being: "It must therefore be known that to know God and to be known by God is the same. We know God and see Him in that He makes us to see and to know. And as the air which illuminates is nothing but what it illuminates, for it shines through this, that it is illuminated: thus do we know that we are known and that He causes Himself to know us."

It is on this foundation that Meister Eckhart builds up his relationship to God. It is a purely spiritual relationship, and it cannot be formed in an image borrowed from the individual life of man. God cannot love His creation as one individual man loves another; God cannot have created the world as a masterbuilder constructs a house. All such thoughts disappear in face of the inner vision. It is in the *nature* of God that He loves the world. A god who could love and also not love is formed in the image of the individual man. "I say in good truth and in eternal truth and in everlasting truth that into every man who has gone within himself God must pour Himself out to the limits of His ability, utterly and completely, so that He retains nothing in His life and in His being, in His nature and in His divinity; everything must He pour out in fruitful fashion." And the inner illumination is something which the soul *necessarily* must find when it goes down into its depths. From this it already becomes evident that the communication of God to mankind cannot be thought of in the image of the *revelation* of one man to another. The *latter* communication can also be left unmade. One man can close himself off from another. God *must* communicate Himself, in conformity with His nature. "It is a certain truth that God must needs seek us, as if all His divinity depended upon it. God can no more do without us than we can do without Him. Although we may turn away from God, yet God can never turn away from us." Consequently the relationship of man to God cannot be understood as containing anything figurative, borrowed from what is *individually* human. Eckhart realizes that part of the accomplishment of the primordial nature of the world is that it should find itself in the human soul. This primordial nature would be imperfect, even unfinished, if it lacked that component of its frame which appears in the human soul. What takes place in man belongs to the primordial nature; and if it did not take place the primordial nature would be only a part of itself. In this sense man can feel himself to be a *necessary* part of the nature of the world. Eckhart expresses this by describing his feelings toward God as follows: "I do not thank God for loving me, for He cannot keep from doing so, whether He wants to or not, His nature compels him to it. . . . Therefore I shall not beg God that He should give me something, nor shall I praise Him for what He has given me. . . . "

But this relationship of the human soul to the primordial nature must not be understood to mean that the soul in its individual character is declared to be one with this primordial nature. The soul which is entangled in the world of the senses, and therewith in the finite, does *not* as such already have the content of the primordial nature within itself. It must first develop it in itself. It must annihilate itself as an individual being. Meister Eckhart has aptly characterized this annihilation as an *"un-becoming"* (*"Entwerdung"*). "When I reach the depths of divinity no one asks me whence I come and where I have been, and no one misses me, for here there is an *un-becoming.*" This relationship is also clearly expressed in the sentence: "I take a basin of water and place a mirror in it and put it under the wheel of the sun. The sun casts its luminous radiance upon the mirror, and yet it is not diminished. The reflection of the mirror in the sun is sun in the sun, and yet the mirror is what it is. Thus it is with God. God is in the soul with His nature and in His being and His divinity, and yet He is not the soul. The reflection of the soul in God is God in God, and yet the soul is what it is."

The soul which gives itself over to the inner illumination recognizes in itself not only what it was *before* the illumination; it also recognizes what it has become only *through* this illumination. "We are to be united with God essentially; we are to be united with God as one; we are to be united with God altogether. How are we to be united with God essentially? This is to be accomplished by a seeing and not by a being. His being cannot be our being, but is to be our life." Not an already existing life —a being *(Wesung)*—is to be understood in the logical sense; but the higher understanding—the seeing—is itself to become life; the spiritual, that which belongs to the idea, is to be experienced by the seeing man in the same way as the individual human nature experiences ordinary, everyday life.

From such starting-points Meister Eckhart also attains a pure *concept of freedom.* In ordinary life the soul is not free. For it is entangled in the realm of lower causes. It accomplishes that to which it is compelled by these lower causes. By the "seeing" it is raised out of the region of these causes. It no longer acts as an individual soul. In it is exposed the primordial essence, which cannot be caused by anything except itself. "God does not compel the will, rather He sets it at liberty, so that it wills nothing but what God Himself wills. And the spirit can will nothing but what God wills; and this is not its unfreedom; it is its true freedom. For freedom is this, that we are not bound, that we be free and pure and unadulterated as we were in our first origin, and when we were wed in the Holy Ghost." It can be said of the enlightened man that he himself is the entity which determines good and evil out of itself. He cannot do otherwise than accomplish the good. For he does not serve the good, rather does the good live within

him. "The righteous man serves neither God nor the creatures, for he is free, and the closer he is to righteousness,
the more he is freedom itself." What then must evil be
for Meister Eckhart? It can only be an acting under the
influence of the lower view, the acting of a soul which
has not passed through the state of un-becoming. Such a
soul is selfish in the sense that it wills only *itself*. Only externally could it bring its willing into harmony with moral
ideals. The seeing soul cannot be selfish in this sense.
Even should it will *itself* it would still will the mastery
of the ideal; for it has made itself into this ideal. It can
no longer will the goals of the lower nature, for it no
longer has anything in common with this lower nature.
It is no compulsion, no deprivation, for the seeing soul to
act in the sense of moral ideals. "For the man who
stands in God's will and in God's love it is a *joy* to do all
the good things God wills, and to leave undone all the evil
things which are against God. And it is impossible for him
to leave a thing undone which God wants to have accomplished. As it would be impossible for one to walk whose
legs are bound, so it would be impossible for one to do ill
who is in God's will." Furthermore Eckhart expressly
protests against an interpretation which would see in his
view a license for anything the individual might want. It is
just in this that one recognizes the seeing man, that he no
longer wants anything as an individual. "Some men say:
If I have God and God's freedom, then I can do everything
I want. They understand these words amiss. As long as
you can do anything which is against God and His commandment, you do not have God's love; you can only

deceive the world into the belief that you have it." Eckhart is convinced that for the soul which goes down into its depths, in these depths a perfect morality will appear, that there all logical understanding and all action in the ordinary sense have an end, and that there an entirely new order of human life begins. "For everything the understanding can grasp, and everything desire demands, is not God. Where understanding and desire have an end, there it is dark, there does God shine. There that power unfolds in the soul which is wider than the wide heavens. . . . The bliss of the righteous and God's bliss is one bliss; for then are the righteous blissful, when God is blissful."

THE FRIENDSHIP WITH GOD

IN JOHANNES TAULER (1300-1361), Heinrich Suso (1295-1366), and Jan van Ruysbroeck (1293-1381) one encounters personalities in whose life and work appear in most impressive manner those movements of the soul which a spiritual path such as that of Meister Eckhart causes in profound natures. If Eckhart seems to be a man who, in the blissful experiencing of spiritual rebirth, speaks of the qualities and nature of knowledge as of a picture he has succeeded in painting, then the others appear as wanderers to whom this rebirth has shown a new road which they mean to walk, but the end of which for them has been removed to an infinite distance. Eckhart describes the splendors of his picture, they the difficulties of the new road. One must be quite clear about man's relationship to his higher insights in order to be able to represent to oneself the difference between such personalities as Eckhart and Tauler. Man is entangled in the world of the senses and in the laws of nature, by which the world of the senses is dominated. He himself is a result of this world. He lives because its forces and substances are active in him, and he perceives and judges this world of the senses in accordance with the laws by which it and he are constructed. When he directs his eye upon an object, not only does the object appear to him as a sum of interacting forces dominated by the laws of nature, but the eye itself is a body constructed according to such laws and forces, and the act of seeing takes place in harmony with these laws and forces. If we had attained the utmost limits of natural science, in all likelihood we could pursue this play of natural forces in accordance with natural laws into the highest regions of the formation of thought.—But in doing this we already rise *above* this play. Do we not stand above all mere conformity to natural laws when we *survey* how we ourselves are integrated into nature? We *see* with our eye in accordance with the laws of nature. But we also *understand* the laws in accordance with which we see. We can stand on a higher elevation and survey simultaneously the external world and ourselves in interplay. Is not then a nature active within us which is higher than the sensory-organic personality which acts according to natural laws and with natural laws? In such activity is there still a partition between our inner world and the external world? That which judges here, which gathers insights, is no longer our individual personality; rather it is the universal essence of the world, which has torn down the barrier between inner world and outer world, and which now embraces both. As it is true that I still remain the same individual in external appearance when I have thus torn down the barrier, so it is true that *in essence* I am no longer this individual. In me now lives the feeling that the universal nature speaks in my soul, the nature which embraces me and the whole world.—Such feelings live in Tauler when he says: "Man is as if he were three men, an animal man, as he is according to the senses, then a rational man, and finally the highest god-like man. . . One is the external, animal sensual man; the other is the internal, rational man, with his rational faculties; the third man is the spirit, the highest part of the soul." (cf. W. Preger, *Geschichte der deutschen Mystik,* History of German Mysticism, Vol. 3, p. 161.) How this third man is superior to the first and second, Eckhart has expressed in the words: "The eye by which I see God is the same eye with which God sees me. My eye and God's eye is one eye and one seeing and one knowing and one feeling." But in Tauler another sentiment lives with this one. He struggles through to a real conception of the spiritual, and does not constantly intermingle the sensory-natural with the spiritual, as do false materialists and false idealists. If Tauler, with his way of thinking, had become a scientist, he would have had to insist that everything natural, including the *whole* man, the first and the second, was to be explained in entirely natural terms. He would never have transferred "purely" spiritual forces into nature. He would not have spoken of a "functionalism" in nature, imagined in accordance with human examples. He knew that where we perceive with the senses no "creative thoughts" are to be found. Instead, there lived in him the strongest consciousness that man is a merely natural being. And since he felt himself to be a curator of the moral life, not a scientist, he felt the contrast which separates this natural being of man

and the seeing of God, which arises in a natural way within the natural, but as something spiritual. It was just in
this contrast that the meaning of life appeared before his
eyes. Man finds himself to be an individual being, a creature of nature. And no science can reveal anything more
to him about this life than that he is such a creature of
nature. As a creature of nature he cannot go beyond the
state appropriate to a creature of nature. He must remain
within it. And yet his inner life leads him beyond it. He
must have confidence in something no science of external
nature can give and show him. If he calls this nature the
existing, he must be able to advance to the view which
acknowledges the non-existing as the higher. Tauler does
not seek a God who exists in the sense of a natural force;
he does not seek a God who has created the world in the
sense of human creations. In him lives the recognition
that even the concept of creation of the teachers of the
Church is only an idealized human creating. It is clear to
him that God is not found in the same manner as science
finds natural processes and natural laws. Tauler is conscious that we cannot simply add God to nature in our
thoughts. He knows that one who thinks God in his sense,
does not have any other content in his thoughts than one
who has grasped nature in thought. Therefore Tauler
does not want to think God; he wants to think divinely.
The knowledge of nature is not *enriched* by knowing
God; it is *transformed*. The knower of God does *not* know
something different from the knower of nature: he *knows
differently*. The knower of God cannot add a single letter

to the knowledge of nature, but through his whole knowledge of nature a new light shines.

What basic sensations dominate the soul of a man who looks at the world from such points of view will depend on how he regards the experience of the soul which spiritual rebirth brings. Within this experience man is wholly a natural being if he looks at himself in interaction with the rest of nature; and he is wholly a spiritual being if he considers the state to which his transformation brings him. One can therefore say with equal justice: The greatest depths of the soul are still natural, and also, They are already divine. Tauler, in conformity with his way of thinking, emphasized the former. No matter how deeply we penetrate into our soul, he said to himself, we always remain individual human beings. But nevertheless, universal nature glows in the depths of the individual soul. Tauler was dominated by the feeling: You cannot detach yourself from individuality, you cannot cleanse yourself of it. Therefore the universal essence cannot appear in you in its purity; it can only shine into the depths of your soul. Thus in these only a reflection, an *image* of the universal essence appears. You can transform your individual personality in such a way that it gives back the image of the universal essence; this universal essence itself does not shine in you. From such conceptions Tauler came to the idea of a Divinity which never entirely merges with the human world, never flows into it. He even expressly insists upon not being confused with those who declare the interior of man to be something divine in itself. He says that the union with God "is taken by ignorant men to occur in the flesh, and they say that they should be transformed into the divine nature; but this is wrong and a mischievous heresy. For even in the highest and most intimate union with God the divine nature and God's essence are high, indeed higher than all height; this leads into a divine abyss, and no creature will ever partake of it." Tauler wants to be deservedly called a believing Catholic, in the sense of his time and of his vocation as a priest. He is not intent upon confronting Christianity with another point of view. He simply wants to deepen and spiritualize Christianity through his views. He speaks of the contents of Scripture as a pious priest. But nevertheless, in his world of ideas the Scriptures become a means of expression for the innermost experiences of the soul. "God accomplishes all His works in the soul and gives them to the soul; and the Father brings forth His only-begotten Son in the soul, as truly as He brings Him forth in eternity, neither less, nor more. What is brought forth when one says: God brings forth in the soul? Is it a similitude of God, or is it an image of God, or is it something of God? No, it is neither image nor similitude of God, but the same God and the same Son whom the Father brings forth in eternity, and nothing but the lovely divine Word, which is the other Person in the Trinity; this does the Father bring forth in the soul . . . and it is from this that the soul has such a great and special dignity." (cf. Preger, *Geschichte der deutschen Mystik,* History of German Mysticism, Vol. 3, p. 219f.)—For Tauler the narratives of the Scriptures become the garment in which he clothes the events of the inner life. "Herod, who drove away the Child and wanted to kill Him, is an image of the world, which still wants to kill this Child in the pious man, wherefore one should and must flee it if one wants to keep the Child alive within oneself, while the Child is the enlightened, believing soul of every man."

Because Tauler directs his attention to the natural man, he is less concerned with describing what happens when the higher man enters into the natural man than with finding the paths which the lower faculties of the personality have to take if they are to be translated into the higher life. As a curator of the moral life he wants to show man the ways to the universal essence. He has absolute faith and confidence that the universal essence will begin to shine in man if the latter so arranges his life that there is a place for the divine in him. But this universal essence can never begin to shine if man shuts himself off in his bare, natural, separate personality. Thus isolated within himself, in the language of Tauler, man is only a part of the world, an individual creature. The more man encloses himself within his existence as part of the world, the less can the universal essence find a place within him. "If man is truly to become one with God, all the faculties of the inner man too must die and be silent. The will must be turned away from even the good and from all willing, and must become will-less." "Man must escape all the senses, turn all his faculties inward, and attain to forgetfulness of all things and of himself." "For the true and eternal word of God is spoken only in the desert, when man has left his own self and all things behind, and stands alone, deserted, and solitary."

When Tauler had reached his highest point the following question came to occupy the center of his mental life: How can man destroy and overcome his individual existence within himself, so that he can take part in life in the sense of the universal life? For one who is in this situation, his feelings toward the universal essence become concentrated in the one thing: reverence for this universal essence, as for that which is inexhaustible and infinite. He says to himself: No matter what level you have attained, there are still higher prospects, still more sublime possibilities. As definite and clear for him as is the direction his steps must take, so clear is it to him that he can never speak of a goal. A new goal is only the beginning of a new road. Through such a new goal man has reached a *degree of development;* the development itself extends into the immeasurable. And what it will achieve on a more distant level it never knows on the present one. There is no *knowing* the final goal; there is only a *trusting* in the road, in the development. There is a knowing of everything man has already achieved. It consists in the pentration of an already existing object by the faculties of our spirit. For the higher inner life *such* a knowing does not exist. Here the faculties of our spirit must first translate the object itself into existence; they must first *create* an existence for it which is like the natural existence. Natural science examines the development of living beings from the simplest to man himself, the most perfect. *This* development lies completed before us. We understand it by penetrating it with our mental faculties. When the development has arrived at man, he does not *find* a further continuation already existing. He himself accomplishes the further development. He now *lives* what he only *knows* for earlier levels. He *creates* objectively what, for that which precedes, he only *re-creates* in line with its spiritual nature. That the truth does not coincide with what exists in nature, but embraces both what exists naturally and what does not exist: Tauler is wholly filled by this in all his sentiments. We are told that he was led to this conviction by an enlightened layman, a "Friend of God from the Oberland." There is a mysterious story in this. There are only conjectures about the place where this Friend of God lived, and about who he was there are not even conjectures. He is said to have heard much about Tauler's manner of preaching, and thereupon to have decided to go to Tauler, who was then a preacher in Strasbourg, in order to fulfill a certain task concerning him. The relationship of Tauler to the Friend of God and the influence which the latter exercised on him are described in a work which is printed together with Tauler's sermons in the oldest editions under the title, *Das Buch des Meisters,* The Book of the Master. In it a Friend of God, in whom the one who entered into relations with Tauler is said to be recognizable, tells of a "master," who has been identified with Tauler himself. He tells how a revolution, a spiritual rebirth, has been brought about in a "master," and how the latter, when he felt his death approaching, called the Friend to him and asked him to write the story of his "enlightenment," but to take care that no one should ever find out who the book deals with. He asks this because all the insights which proceed from him are yet not of him. "For know that God has performed everything through me, poor worm that I am, and thus it is not mine, but God's." A scholarly dispute which has developed in connection with this matter is not of the least importance as far as its essentials are concerned. On the one side (Denifle, *Die Dichtungen des Gottesfreundes im Oberlande*, The Writings of the Friend of God in the Oberland) the attempt has been made to prove that the Friend of God never existed, that his existence was invented, and that the books attributed to him originated with someone else (Rulman Merswin). Wilhelm Preger (*Geschichte der deutschen Mystik*, History of German Mysticism) has endeavored with many reasons to support this existence, the genuineness of the writings, and the correctness of the facts relating to Tauler.—It is not incumbent upon me here to illuminate by obtrusive research a human relationship of which one who knows how to read the relevant writings knows full well that it is to remain a secret. (These relevant writings, among others, are: *Von eime eiginwilligen weltwisen manne, der von eime heiligen weltpriestere gewiset wart uffe demuetige gehorsamme,* Of a self-willed worldly-wise Man who was shown the Way to Humble Obedience by a holy secular Priest, 1338; *Das Buch von den zwei Mannen,* The Book of the Two Men; *Der gefangene Ritter,* The Captured Knight, 1349; *Die geistliche stege,* The Spiritual Stairs, 1350; *Von der geistlichen Leiter,* Of the Spiritual Ladder, 1357; *Das Meisterbuch,* The Book of the Master, 1369; *Geschichte von zwei jun-*

gen 15jährigen Knaben, Story of Two Young 15-Year-Old Boys.) It is entirely sufficient to say of Tauler that at a certain stage of his life a change such as the one I am about to describe occurred in him. Here Tauler's personality is no longer in question, but rather a personality "in general." As regards Tauler we are only concerned with the fact that we have to understand the transformation in *him* from the point of view indicated below. If we compare his later activity with his earlier, the fact of this transformation is immediately evident. I omit all external circumstances and relate the inner soul processes of the "master" under "the influence of the layman." What my reader imagines the "layman" and the "master" to be, depends entirely upon the disposition of his spirit; I do not know that what I myself imagine them to be is applicable to anyone else.—A master instructs his listeners about the relationship of the soul to the universal essence of things. He speaks of the fact that man no longer feels the natural, limited faculties of the individual personality to be active within him when he descends into the profound depths of his soul. There it is no longer the individual man who speaks; it is God. There man does not see God, or the world; there God sees Himself. Man has become *one* with God. But the master knows that this teaching has not yet fully come to life within him. He thinks it with the intellect, but he does not yet live within it with every fiber of his personality. Thus he teaches about a state which he has not yet fully experienced within himself. The description of this state corresponds to the truth, but this truth is worth nothing if it does not acquire life, if it does not bring itself forth as existence in the real world. The "lay-man" or "Friend of God" hears of the master and his teachings. He is not less penetrated with the truth the master utters than is the latter himself. But he does not possess this truth as a thing of the intellect. He possesses it as the whole force of his life. He knows that one can utter this truth when it has come to one from the outside, without living in its sense in the least. In that case one has nothing within oneself beyond the natural understanding of the intellect. One then speaks of this natural under-standing as though it were the highest, identical with the action of the universal essence. This is not so, because it was not acquired in a life which, when it approached this knowledge, was already transformed and reborn. What one acquires as a *merely* natural man remains *merely* nat-ural, even if later one expresses the main feature of the higher knowledge in words. The transformation must come out of nature itself. Nature, which in living has de-veloped to a certain stage, must be developed further by life; something new must come into being through this further development. Man must not merely look back upon the development which has already taken place, and consider as the highest what is *re-formed* in his mind con-cerning this development; he must *look forward* to what has not yet been created; his knowledge must be the *be-ginning* of a new content, not an *end* of the content of the previous development. Nature advances from worm to mammal, from mammal to man in a real, not in a con-ceptual process. Man is not merely to repeat this process in spirit. The spiritual repetition is only the beginning of a new real development, which, however, is a spiritual reality. Man then understands not merely what nature has brought forth; he carries nature further; he transforms his understanding into living action. He brings forth the spirit within himself, and from then on this spirit advances from one stage of development to another, just as nature advances. The spirit initiates a natural process on a higher level. When one who has understood this speaks about the God who sees Himself within man, this speaking takes on another character. He attaches little value to the fact that an insight already obtained has led him into the depths of the universal essence, but his spiritual disposition acquires a new character. It continues to develop in the direction determined by the universal essence. Such a man not only *looks* at the world in a different way from one who is merely rational: he *lives* his life differently. He does not speak of the *sense* which life already has through the forces and laws of the world; rather he gives a new sense to this life. No more than the fish has in itself what appears as mammal at a later stage of development, does the rational man already have in himself what is to be born out of him as a higher man. If the fish could understand itself and the things around it, it would regard being a fish as the sense of life. It would say: The universal essence is like the fish; in the fish the universal essence sees itself. Thus the fish might speak as long as it merely holds fast to its intellectual understanding. In reality it does not hold fast to it. In its actions it goes beyond its understanding. It becomes a reptile, and later a mammal. In reality the sense it gives to itself goes beyond the sense which

mere reflection suggests to it. Thus must it also be with
man. In reality he gives himself a sense; he does not stop
at the sense he already has, and which reflection shows him.
Understanding leaps beyond itself, if only it understands
itself aright. Understanding cannot derive the world from
an already completed God; from a germ, it can only develop in a direction toward a God. The man who has understood this does not want to look at God as something
that is outside of him; he wants to treat God as a Being
that walks with him toward a goal which, at the outset, is
as unknown as the nature of the mammal is unknown to
the fish. He does not want to be the knower of the hidden
or self-revealing, existing God, but the friend of the divine action and operation, which is superior to existence
and non-existence. The layman who came to the master
was a "Friend of God" in this sense. And through him the
master was transformed from a contemplator of the nature of God into "one who lives in the spirit," who not
merely contemplated, but *lived* in the higher sense. Now
the latter no longer brought concepts and ideas of the intellect from within himself; these concepts and ideas
sprang from him as living, real spirit. He no longer merely edified his listeners; he moved them deeply. He no
longer plunged their souls within themselves; he led them
into a new life. This is told us symbolically: through the
effect of his sermon about forty people fell down and were
as if dead.

A leader into such a new life is represented by a work,
the author of which is unknown. Luther first made it

known by having it published. The philologist, Franz
Pfeiffer recently reprinted it from a manuscript of the
year 1497, with a translation in modern German facing
the original text. The introduction to the work announces
its intention and its goal: "Here the Frankfurter begins
and says exceedingly high and beautiful things of a con-
summate life." This is followed by "the preface concerning the Frankfurter:" "This booklet the omnipotent, eternal God has uttered through a wise, judicious, truthful,
righteous man, his friend, who was formerly a Teutonic
Knight, a priest and a custodian in the house of the Teutonic Knights in Frankfurt; it teaches many lovely insights
into divine truth, and especially how and by what one can
recognize the true and righteous Friends of God, and also
the unrighteous, false, free spirits, who do much harm to
the holy Church."—By "free spirits" one is to understand those who live in a world of ideas like that of the
"master" described above before his transformation by
the "Friend of God," and by the "true and righteous
Friends of God" those with the way of thinking of the
"layman." One can further ascribe to the book the intention of acting upon its readers in the same way as the
"Friend of God from the Oberland" acted upon the master. One does not know the author. But what does this
mean? One does not know when he was born and when
he died, and what he did in the external life. That the
author wanted these facts of his outer life to remain forever secret is something which belongs to the way he
wanted to act. Not the "self" of this or that man, born at a
certain time, is to speak to us, but the selfhood on the basis

of which the "particularity of individualities" (in the sense of the words of Paul Asmus, cf. p. 116 above) first develops. "If God were to take unto himself all men who are now and who have ever been, and were to become man in them, and were they to become God in Him, and if it did not happen in me too, my fall and my estrangement would never be remedied, unless indeed it happened also in me. And in this restoration and improvement I can and should do nothing but merely and purely suffer what is done, so that God alone does and accomplishes everything within me, and I suffer Him and all His works and His divine Will. But if I do not want to suffer this, and possess myself in attributes of the self, that is in My and I, in Me and the like, then God is hindered, so that He cannot, pure and alone and without obstacle, accomplish His work within me. Therefore also my fall and my estrangement remain unremedied." The "Frankfurter" does not wish to speak as an individual; he wants to let God speak. Of course he knows that he can only do this as an individual, separate personality, but he is a "Friend of God," that is, a man who does not want to depict the nature of life through contemplation, but who wants to point out, through the living spirit, the *beginning* of an avenue of development. The discussions in the book represent various instructions on how this road is to be attained. The basic idea always returns: man is to cast off everything connected with the view that makes him appear as an individual, separate personality. This idea seems to be carried out only with respect to the moral life; it must also be applied to the life of higher understanding. One must destroy in oneself what appears as separateness, then the separate existence ceases; the all-life enters into us. We cannot possess ourselves of this all-life by drawing it to us. It comes into us when we silence the separate existence within us. We possess the all-life least just when we regard our individual existence as if the All already reposed within it. The latter only appears in the individual existence when this individual existence does not claim that it is something. The book calls this claim of the individual existence the "assumption" *(Annehmen)*. Through the "assumption" the "self" makes it impossible for the all-life to enter into it. The self then puts itself as a part, as something incomplete, in the place of the whole, of the complete. "The complete is a being which comprises and embraces all beings in itself and in its being, and without and outside which there is no true being, and in which all things have their being; for it is the being of all things and is in itself unchangeable and immovable, and changes and moves all other things. But the divided and incomplete is what has sprung from the complete, or which it becomes, just like a brilliance or a shining which flows from the sun or from a light and appears as something, as this or that. And this is called creature, and none of these divided ones is identical with the complete. *And therefore the complete also is not identical with any of the divided ones.* . . . When the complete appears one rejects what is divided. But when does it come? I say: When, insofar as it is possible, it is known, felt, and tasted in the soul; for the lack is wholly in us and not in it. For just as the sun illuminates the whole world and is as close to one man as to another, a blind man nevertheless does not see it. But that is not a defect in the sun, but in the blind man. . . . If my eye is to see something it must be cleansed of, or freed from, all other things. . . . One might want to ask: Insofar as it is unknowable and incomprehensible for all creatures, and the soul is a creature, how can it be known in the soul? Answer: Therefore it is that one says that the creature is to be known *as a creature.*" This is as much as to say that all that is creature is to be regarded as creature-ness and as created, and is not to regard itself as an I and as selfhood, which latter makes this knowing impossible. "For in that creature in which the complete is to be known, creatureness, being created, I, selfhood and the like must be lost and come to nothing." (Chapter I of the work of the Frankfurter.) Thus the soul must look into itself; there it will find its I, its selfhood. If it stops at this, it separates itself from the complete. If it regards its selfhood only as something loaned to it, as it were, and destroys it in spirit, it will be seized by the stream of the all-life, of the complete. "If the creature takes on something good, such as being, life, knowledge, insight, capacity, in short all that one should call good, and deems that it itself is this or that this belongs to it, the creature, or is of it: as often and to the extent that this happens, it turns itself away." There are "two eyes in the created soul of man. One is the possibility of looking into eternity; the other, of looking into time and into the creature." "Man should thus stand and be free without himself, that is without selfhood, I, Me, My and the like, so that he seeks and purposes himself and what is his as little in all things as if it did not exist; and he should also estimate himself as little as if he did not exist, and as if another had performed all his works." (Chapter 15.) With relation to the author of these sentences too it must be considered that the conceptual content to which he gives a direction through his higher ideas and feelings is that of a pious priest of his time. Here it is not a matter of the conceptual content, but of the direction; not of the ideas, but of the spiritual disposition. One who does not live in Christian dogmas as this author does, but rather in concepts of natural science, imprints other ideas on his sentences; but with these other ideas he points in the same direction. And this direction is what leads to the overcoming of selfhood through this selfhood itself. It is in his self that the highest light shines for man. But this light only gives the right reflection to his world of ideas when man is aware that it is not the light of his self, but the universal light of the world. Therefore there is no more important knowledge than self-knowledge; and at the same time there is none which so completely leads beyond itself. When the "self" knows itself aright it is already no longer a "self." In his words the author of the book under discussion expresses this as follows: "For God's nature is without this and without that and without selfhood and I; but the nature and peculiarity of the creature is that it seeks and wills itself and what belongs to it, and the "this" and "that"; and from everything it does or leaves undone it wants to receive profit and advantage. But where the creature or man loses his own being and his selfhood and himself, and goes out of himself, there God enters with His own Being, that is with His Selfhood." (Chapter 24.) Man ascends from a conception of his "self" in which the latter appears to him as his *essence,* to one where he sees it as a mere organ in which the universal essence acts upon itself. In line with the ideas of our book it is said: "If man can reach the point where he belongs as much to God as a man's hand belongs to him, then let him rest content and seek no further." (Chapter 54.) This is not to say that man should stop at a certain point of his development; rather, when he has come as far as is indicated in the words above, he should no longer pursue investigations about the meaning of the hand, but rather use the hand, so that it can serve the body to which it belongs.—

Heinrich Suso and Jan van Ruysbroeck had a spiritual disposition which can be described as genius of soul. Their feelings are drawn by something resembling instinct to the point to which Eckhart's and Tauler's feelings were led through a higher life of ideas. Suso's heart turns ardently toward a primordial essence which embraces the individual man as well as the whole remaining world, and in which, forgetting himself, he wants to be absorbed like a drop of water in the great ocean. He speaks of this yearning for the universal essence not as of something which he wants to grasp in his thoughts, but he speaks of it as of a natural impulse which makes his soul drunk with the desire for the annihilation of his separate existence and for the rebirth in the all-embracing activity of the infinite essence. "Turn your eyes to the being in its pure and bare simplicity, so that you may abandon this and that partial being. Take only being in itself, which is unmixed with non-being, for all non-being denies all being; thus the being in itself also denies all non-being. A thing which is still to become, or has been, does not exist now in its essential presence. Mixed being or non-being can however be recognized only by the aid of a mark of the universal being. For if one wants to understand a thing the reason is first met by being, and that is a being which effects all things. It is not a divided being of this or that creature, for the divided being is ever mingled with the otherness of a possibility of receiving something. Therefore the nameless divine being must in itself be a universal being, which sustains all divided beings with its presence." Thus speaks Suso in the autobiography which he composed with the aid of his disciple, Elsbet Stäglin. He too is a pious priest and lives wholly in the Christian realm of ideas. He lives in it as if it were completely unthinkable for someone with his spiritual *direction* to live in a different spiritual *world*. But of him too it is true that one can combine another conceptual content with his spiritual direction. This is clearly indicated by the way the content of the Christian doctrine becomes an inner experience for him, while his relationship to Christ becomes one between his spirit and the eternal truth, of a purely conceptual-spiritual kind. He has written a *Büchlein von der ewigen Weisheit*, Little Book of Eternal Wisdom. In this he lets the "eternal wisdom" speak to its "servant," that is, presumably, to himself: "Do you not recognize me? How is it you are even sunk down, or has consciousness deserted you because of your great distress, my tender child? It is I, compassionate wisdom, who have opened wide the depths of bottomless compassion, which is even hidden to all the saints, in order to receive you and all repentant hearts in kindness; it is I, the sweet, eternal wisdom, who became poor and miserable in order to bring you back to your dignity; it is I who suffered bitter death in order to bring you back to life! Here I stand, pale and bloody and loving, as I stood by the high gallows of the Cross, between the strict judgment of my Father and you. It is I, your brother; look, it is I, your spouse! Everything you ever did against me I have utterly forgotten, as if it had never happened, if only you now turn completely to me and do not part from me again." For Suso, everything material-temporal in the Christian conception of the world has, as one can see, become a spiritual-ideal process within his soul.— From some chapters of the above-mentioned autobiography of Suso it might appear as if he had let himself be led not by the mere activity of his own spiritual faculties, but by external revelations, by spirit-like visions. But he clearly expresses his opinion on this. One attains the truth only by exercise of reason, not through some revelation. "The difference between pure truth and doubtful visions in the professing substance . . . I shall also tell you. A direct seeing of the bare Divinity is the right, pure truth, without any doubt; and any vision is the nobler the more reasonable and imageless it is, and the more like this bare seeing."—Meister Eckhart also leaves no doubt that he rejects the view which sees the spiritual in substantial-spatial forms, in apparitions that can be perceived in the same way as sensory ones. Thus spirits like Suso and Eckhart are opponents of a view such as that which expresses itself in the Spiritualism that developed in the 19th century.

Jan van Ruysbroeck, the Belgian mystic, walked the same paths as Suso. His spiritual road found a spirited opponent in Jean de Gerson (born 1363), who was for some time Chancellor of the University of Paris, and played an important role at the Council of Constance. It throws some light on the nature of the mysticism cultivated by Tauler, Suso, and Ruysbroeck if one compares it with the mystical endeavors of Gerson, whose predecessors were Richard of St. Victor, Bonaventura, and others.—Ruysbroeck himself fought against those whom he counted among the heretical mystics. The latter he considered all who, on the basis of an unconsidered intellectual judgment, hold all things to be the amanation of *one* primordial essence, and who thus see in the world a diversity only, and in God the unity of this diversity. Ruysbroeck did not count himself among these, for he knew that one cannot reach the primordial essence by a contemplation of things themselves, but only by raising oneself from this lower to a higher way of thinking. Similarly he turned against those who without further ado wanted to see in the individual man, in his separate existence (in his creature-ness), his higher nature also. He much lamented the error which effaces all differences in the world of the senses, and lightly says that things are different only in appearance, while in essence they are all the same. For a way of thinking such as Ruysbroeck's this would be just as if one were to say: That for our eyes the trees of an avenue converge in the distance does not concern us. In reality they are everywhere equally distant, therefore our eyes must accustom themselves to seeing correctly. But our eyes do see correctly. That the trees converge is due to a necessary law of nature, and we should not object to our way of seeing, but rather understand in the *mind* why we see *thus*. The mystic too does not turn away from the things of the senses. He accepts them as being sensory, as they are. And it is also clear to him that they cannot become other through any intellectual judgment. But in the spirit he goes beyond the senses and beyond reason, and only then does he find unity. He has an unshakeable *belief* that he can develop to the point of seeing this unity. Therefore he ascribes to human nature the divine spark which can be made to shine in him, *to shine of itself*. It is different with spirits of Gerson's kind. They do *not* believe in this *shining of itself*. For them what men can see always remains something external, which must come to them externally from one side or another. Ruysbroeck believed that the highest wisdom must become apparent to the mystical seeing; Gerson believed only that the soul could illuminate the content of an external teaching (that of the Church). For Gerson mysticism was nothing but one's having a warm feeling for everything which is revealed in the content of this teaching. For Ruysbroeck it was a belief that all content of this teaching is also born in the soul. Therefore Gerson reproves Ruysbroeck for imagining not only that he possesses the capacity to see the universal essence with clearness, but that an activity of the universal essence manifests itself in this seeing.

Ruysbroeck simply could not be understood by Gerson. They were speaking of two totally different things. Ruysbroeck has his eye fixed on that life of the soul which lives its God; Gerson sees only a life of the soul which wants to love a God whom it never will be able to live within itself. Like so many others Gerson too fought against something which was foreign to him only because it could not be fitted into his experience[1]).

---

[1] See Addendum II.

CARDINAL NICOLAS OF CUSA

A GLORIOUSLY SHINING STAR in the firmament of medieval spiritual life is Nicolas Chrypffs of Cusa (near Treves, 1401-1464). He stands upon the heights of the learning of his time. In mathematics he has produced outstanding work. In natural science he may be described as the precursor of Copernicus, for he held the point of view that the earth is a moving heavenly body like others. He had already broken with the view on which the great astronomer, Tycho Brahe, still relied a hundred years later when he flung the following sentence against the teaching of Copernicus: "The earth is a coarse and heavy mass, unsuited for movement; how can Copernicus make a star of it and lead it around in the atmosphere?" Nicolas of Cusa, who not only encompassed the knowledge of his time but developed it further, also to a high degree had the capacity of awakening this knowledge to an inner life, so that it not only elucidates the external world but also procures for man that spiritual life for which he must long from the most profound depths of his soul. If one compares Nicolas with such spirits as Eckhart or Tauler, one reaches an important conclusion. Nicolas is the scientific thinker who wants to raise himself to a higher view as the result of his research into the things of the world; Eckhart and Tauler are the believing confessors who seek the higher life through the contents of their faith. Nicolas finally reaches the same inner life as Meister Eckhart, but the content of the inner life of the former is a rich learning. The full meaning of the difference becomes clear when one considers that for one who interests himself in the various sciences there is a real danger of misjudging the scope of the way of knowing which elucidates the different fields of learning. Such a person can easily be misled into the belief that there is only one way of knowing. He will then either under- or over-estimate this knowing, which leads to the goal in things pertaining to the different sciences. In the one case he will approach objects of the highest spiritual life in the same way as a problem in physics, and deal with them in terms of concepts that he uses to deal with the force of gravity and with electricity. According to whether he considers himself to be more or less enlightened, to him the world becomes a blindly acting mechanism, an organism, the functional construction of a personal God, or perhaps a structure directed and penetrated by a more or less clearly imagined "world soul." In the other case he notices that the particular knowledge of which he has experience is useful only for the things of the sensory world; then he becomes a skeptic who says to himself: we cannot know anything about the things which lie beyond the world of the senses. Our knowledge has a boundary. As far as the needs of the higher life are concerned, we can only throw ourselves into the arms of a faith untouched by knowledge. For a learned theologian like Nicolas of Cusa, who was at the same time a natural scientist, the second danger was especially real. In his education he was after all a product of Scholasticism, the dominant philosophy in the scholarly life of the Church of the Middle Ages, which had been brought to its highest flower by Thomas Aquinas (1225-1274), the "Prince of Scholastics." This philosophy must be used as a background if one wants to depict the personality of Nicolas of Cusa.

Scholasticism is in the highest degree a product of human ingenuity. In it the logical faculty celebrated its greatest triumphs. One who aims to elaborate concepts in their sharpest and clearest contours should serve an apprenticeship with the Scholastics. It is they who provide the highest schooling for the technique of thinking. They have an incomparable agility in moving in the field of pure thought. It is easy to underestimate what they were capable of accomplishing in this field. For in most areas of learning the latter is accessible to man only with difficulty. Most people attain it clearly only in the realms of counting, of arithmetic, and in thinking about the properties of geometric forms. We can count by adding a unit to a number in our thoughts, without calling sensory images to our help. We also calculate without such images, in the pure element of thought alone. As for geometric forms, we know that they do not completely coincide with any sensory image. In the reality of the senses there exists no (conceptual) circle. And yet our thinking occupies itself with the latter. For objects and processes which are more complicated than numerical and spatial structures, it is more difficult to find conceptual counter-parts. This has led to the claim made in some quarters that there is only as much real knowledge in the various fields of investigation as there is that in them which can be measured and counted. This is as decidedly wrong as is anything one-sided; but it seduces many, as often only something one-sided can. Here the truth is that most people are not capable of grasping purely conceptual when it is no longer a matter of something measurable or countable. But one who cannot do this in connection with higher realms of life and knowledge resembles in this respect a child who has not yet learned to count in any other way than by adding one pea to another. The thinker who said that there is as much true knowledge in any field of learning as there is mathematics in it, did not grasp the full truth of the matter. One must require that everything which cannot be measured and counted, is to be treated in the same conceptual fashion as numerical and spatial structures. And this requirement was respected by the Scholastics in the highest degree. Everywhere they sought the conceptual content of things, just as the mathematician seeks it in the area of the measurable and countable.

In spite of this accomplished logical skill the Scholastics attained only a one-sided and subordinate concept of cognition. According to this concept, in the process of cognition man produces in himself an image of what he is to grasp. It is quite obvious that with such a concept of cognition, one must place all reality outside of cognition. For in the process of cognition one cannot then grasp a thing itself, but *only an image* of this thing. Man also cannot grasp himself in his self-knowledge; what he grasps of himself is only an image of his self. It is quite in the spirit of Scholasticism that someone who is closely acquainted with it says (K. Werner in his *Franz Suarez und die Scholastik der letzten Jahrhunderte,* Francisco Suarez and the Scholasticism of the Last Centuries, p. 122): "In time man has no perception of his self, the hidden foundation of his spiritual nature and life; . . . he will never be able to look at himself; for either, forever estranged from God, he will find in himself only a bottomless dark abyss and endless emptiness, or he will, blessed in God, and turning his gaze inward, find only God, Whose sun of grace shines within him, and Whose *image* reflects itself in the spiritual traits of his nature." One who thinks about all cognition in this way has only a concept of that cognition which is applicable to external things. What is sensory in a thing always remains external to us. Therefore into our cognition we can only receive images of what is sensory in the world. When we perceive a color or a stone we cannot ourselves become color or stone in order to know the nature of the color or of the stone. And neither can the color or the stone transform itself into a part of our own nature! But it must be asked, Is the concept of such a cognition, focused as it is upon the external in things, an exhaustive one?—It is true that for Scholasticism all human cognition coincides *in its essentials* with *this* cognition. Another writer who knows Scholasticism extremely well, (Otto Willmann, in his *Geschichte des Idealismus,* History of Idealism, V. 2, 2nd ed., p. 396) characterizes the concept of cognition of this philosophy in the following way: "Our spirit, associated with the body as it is in earthly life, is primarily directed toward the surrounding world of matter, but focused upon the spiritual in it; that is, the essences, natures, and forms of things, the elements of existence which are akin to it and provide it with the rungs by which it ascends to the supra-sensory; the field of our cognition is thus the realm of experience, but we should learn to understand what it offers, penetrate to its sense and idea, and thereby open to ourselves the world of ideas." The Scholastic could not attain a different concept of cognition. He was prevented from doing so by the dogmatic teaching of his theology. If he had fixed his spiritual eye upon what he considered to be a mere image, he would have seen that the spiritual content of things reveals itself in this supposed image; he would then have found that God does not merely *reflect* Himself within him, but that He *lives* in him, is present in him in His essence. In looking within himself he would not have beheld a dark abyss, an endless emptiness, nor merely an image of God; rather would he have felt that a life pulses in him which is the divine life itself, and that his own life is the life of God. This the Scholastic could not admit. In his opinion God could not enter into him and speak out of him; He could only exist in him as an image. In reality, the Divinity had to be presupposed outside the self. Thus it had to *reveal* itself through supernatural communications from the outside, and could not do so within, through the spiritual life. But what is intended by this is exactly what is least achieved. It is the highest possible concept of the Divinity which is to be attained. In reality, the Divinity is degraded to a thing among other things, but these other things reveal themselves to man in a natural manner, through experience, while the Divinity is to reveal Itself to him supernaturally. However, a difference between the cognition of the Divine and of the creation is made in saying that, as concerns the creation, the external thing is given in the experience, that one has *knowledge* of it. As concerns the Divine, the object is not given in the experience; one can only attain it through *faith*. Thus for the Scholastic the highest things are not objects of knowledge, but only of faith. It is true that, according to the Scholastic view, the relationship of knowledge to faith is not to be imagined in such a way that in a certain field *only* knowledge reigns, in another *only* faith. For "cognition of the existing is possible for us, because it originates in a creative cognition; things are *for* the spirit because they are *from* the spirit; they tell us something because they have a meaning which a higher intelligence has put into them." (O. Willmann, *Geschichte des Idealismus,* History of Idealism, V. 2, p. 383.) Since God has created the world according to His ideas, if we grasp the ideas of the world, we can also grasp the traces of the Divine in the world through scientific reflection. But what God is in His essence we can only grasp through the revelation which He has given us in a supernatural manner, and in which we must believe. What we must think concerning the highest things is not decided

by any human knowledge, but by faith; and "to faith
belongs everything that is contained in the Scriptures of
the New and Old Covenant, and in the divine traditions."
(Joseph Kleutgen, *Die Theologie der Vorzeit,* The Theology of Antiquity, V. 1, p. 39.)—We cannot make it our
task here to describe in detail and to explain the relationship of the content of faith to that of knowledge. In
reality, the content of all faith originates in an inner experience man has had at some time. It is then preserved,
according to its external import, without the consciousness
of how it was acquired. It is said of it that it came into the
world through supernatural revelation. The content of the
Christian faith was simply accepted by the Scholastics as
tradition. Science and inner experience were not allowed
to claim any rights over it. Scholasticism could no more
permit itself to create a concept of God than science can
create a tree; it had to accept the revealed concept as given,
just as natural science accepts the tree as given. The Scholastic could never admit that the spiritual itself shines and
lives within man. He therefore drew a limit to the jurisdiction of science where the field of external experience ends.
Human cognition could not be permitted to produce a
concept of the higher entities out of itself. It was to accept
a revealed one. That in doing this it actually only accepted one which had been produced at an earlier stage
of human spiritual life, and declared it to be a revealed
one, this the Scholastics could not admit.—In the course
of the development of Scholasticism therefore, all those
ideas had disappeared from it which still indicated the
manner in which man has produced the concepts of the

Divine in a natural way. In the first centuries of the development of Christianity, at the time of the Fathers of
the Church, we see how the content of the teachings of
theology came into being little by little through the in-
clusion of inner experiences. This content is still treated
entirely as an inner experience by Joannes Scotus Erigena,
who stood at the height of Christian theological learning
in the ninth century. Among the Scholastics of the succeeding centuries this quality of an inner experience is
completely lost; the old content is reinterpreted as the content of an external, supernatural revelation.—One can
therefore interpret the activity of the mystical theologians
Eckhart, Tauler, Suso and their companions by saying:
They were inspired by the content of the teachings of the
Church, which is contained in theology, but had been reinterpreted, to bring forth a similar content out of themselves anew as an inner experience.

*

Nicolas of Cusa enters upon the task of ascending by
oneself to inner experiences from the knowledge one
acquires in the different sciences. There can be no doubt
that the excellent logical technique the Scholastics had
developed and for which Nicolas had been educated, fur-
nishes an excellent means for attaining inner experiences,
although the Scholastics themselves were kept from this
road by their positive faith. But one will only understand
Nicolas completely when one considers that his vocation
as priest, which raised him to the dignity of Cardinal, prevented him from making a complete break with the faith

of the Church, which found its contemporary expression in Scholastic theology. We find him so far advanced along a certain path that every further step would of necessity have led him out of the Church. Therefore we understand the Cardinal best if we complete that step which he did not take, and then in retrospect illuminate what had been his intention.

The most important concept of the spiritual life of Nicolas is that of "learned ignorance." By this he understands a cognition which represents a higher level, as opposed to ordinary knowledge. Knowledge in the subordinate sense is the grasping of an object by the spirit. The most important characteristic of knowledge is that it gives information about something outside the spirit, that is, that it looks at something which it itself is not. In knowledge, the spirit thus is occupied with things thought of as being outside of it. But what the spirit forms in itself concerning things is the *essence* of things. Things are spirit. At first man sees the spirit only through the sensory covering. What remains outside the spirit is only this sensory covering; the essence of things enters into the spirit. When the spirit then looks upon this essence, which is substance of its substance, it can no longer speak of knowledge, for it does not look upon a thing which is outside of it; it looks upon a thing which is a part of itself; it looks upon itself. It no longer knows; it only looks upon itself. It is not concerned with a "knowing," but with a *"not-knowing."* It no longer *grasps* something through the spirit; it "beholds, without grasping," its own life. This highest level of cognition, in relation to the lower levels, is a "not-knowing."—It will be seen that the *essence* of things can only be communicated through this level of cognition. With his "learned not-knowing" Nicolas of Cusa thus speaks of nothing but the knowledge reborn as inner experience. He himself tells how he came to have this inner experience. "I made many attempts to unite my thoughts about God and the world, about Christ and the Church in one fundamental idea, but of them all none satisfied me until finally, during the return from Greece by sea, the gaze of my spirit lifted itself, as if through an inspiration from on high, to the view in which God appeared to me as the highest unity of all contrasts." To a greater or lesser extent the influences which derive from a study of his predecessors are involved in this inspiration. In his way of thinking one recognizes a peculiar renewal of the ideas we encounter in the writing of a certain Dionysius. Scotus Erigena, mentioned above, had translated this work into Latin. He calls the author "the great and divine revealer." These writings were first mentioned in the first half of the sixth century. They were ascribed to that Dionysius the Aeropagite mentioned in the *Acts of the Apostles,* who was converted to Christianity by Paul. Here we shall not go into the problem as to when these writings were really composed. Their contents had a strong effect on Nicolas, as they already had on Joannes Scotus Erigena, and as they must also have been stimulating in many respects for the way of thinking of Eckhart and his companions. The "learned not-knowing" is prefigured in a certain way in these writings. Here we shall record only the main feature of the way of thinking of these writings.

Man first comes to know the things of the sensory world. He reflects on their existence and activity. The primordial foundation of all things must lie higher than the things themselves. Man therefore cannot expect to grasp this primordial foundation with the same concepts and ideas as he grasps the things themselves. If therefore he attributes to the primordial foundation (God) qualities which he knows from lower things, these qualities can only be auxiliary ideas of the weak spirit, which draws the primordial foundation down to itself in order to be able to imagine it. In reality, therefore, no quality which lower things have can be said to belong to God. It cannot even be said that God *is*. For "being" too is a concept which man has formed in connection with lower things. But God is exalted above "being" and "not-being." Thus the God to Whom we ascribe qualities is not the true one. We arrive at the true God if we imagine a "Supergod" above a God with such qualities. Of this "Supergod" we can know nothing in the ordinary sense. In order to reach Him, "knowing" must flow into "not-knowing."—One can see that such a view is based on the consciousness that out of what his sciences have furnished him man himself—in a purely natural way —can develop a higher cognition, which is no longer *mere knowledge*. The Scholastic view declared knowledge to be incapable of such a development, and at the point where knowledge is supposed to end, it had faith, based on an external revelation, come to the aid of knowledge.—Nicolas of Cusa thus was on the way toward once again developing *that* out of knowledge which the Scholastics had declared to be unattainable for cognition.

From the point of view of Nicolas of Cusa therefore, one cannot say that there is only *one* kind of cognition. Cognition, on the contrary, is clearly divided into what mediates a knowledge of external things, and what is itself the object of which one acquires knowledge. The former kind of cognition rules in the sciences which we acquire concerning the things and processes of the sensory world; the latter kind is in us when we ourselves *live* in what has been acquired. The second kind of cognition develops from the first. Yet it is the same world to which both kinds of cognition refer, and it is the same man who shares in both. The question must arise, How does it come about that one and the same man develops two kinds of cognition of one and the same world?—The direction in which the answer to this question is to be sought was already indicated in our discussion of Tauler (cf. p. 151). Here this answer can be formulated even more definitely with regard to Nicolas of Cusa. First of all, man lives as a separate (individual) being among other separate beings. To the influences which the other beings exercise upon one another, in him is added the faculty of (lower) cognition. Through his senses he receives impressions of the other beings, and he works upon these impressions with his spiritual faculties. He directs his spiritual gaze away from external things and looks at himself, at his own activity. Thus self-knowledge arises in him. As long as he remains upon this level of self-knowledge he does not yet look upon himself in the true sense of the word. He can still believe that there is some hidden entity active within him, and that what appears to him as *his* activity are only the manifestations and actions of this entity. But the point can come at which it becomes clear to man through an incontrovertible inner experience that in what he perceives and experiences within himself he possesses, not the manifestation, the action, of a hidden force or entity, but this entity itself in its primordial form. He can then say to himself: All other things I encounter in a way ready-made, and I, who stand outside them, add to them what the spirit has to say with regard to them. But in what I myself thus creatively add to things in myself, in that I myself live, that is what I am, that is my own essence. But what is it that speaks in the depths of my spirit? It is knowledge that speaks, the knowledge I have acquired about the things of the world. But in this knowledge it is not some action, some manifestation which speaks; something speaks which keeps nothing back of what it has in itself. In *this* knowledge speaks the world in all its immediacy. But I have acquired this knowledge from things and from myself, as from a thing among things. Out of my own essence it is I myself and the things who speak. In reality I no longer merely express my nature; I express the nature of things. My "I" is the form, the organ through which things declare themselves with regard to themselves. I have gained the experience that I experience my own essence within myself, and for me this experience becomes enlarged into another, that in me and through me the universal essence expresses itself, or, in other words, knows itself. Now I can no longer feel myself to be a thing among things; I can only feel myself to be a form in which the universal essence has its life.—It is therefore only natural that one and the same man should have two kinds of cognition. With regard to the sensory facts he is a thing among things, and, insofar as this is the case, he acquires a knowledge of these things; but at any moment he can have the higher experience that he is the form in which the universal essence looks upon itself. Then he himself is transformed from a thing among things into a form of the universal essence—and with him the knowledge of things is changed into an utterance of the nature of things. This transformation however can in fact be accomplished only by man himself. What is mediated in the higher cognition is not yet present as long as this higher cognition itself is not present. It is only in creating this higher cognition that man develops his nature, and only through the higher cognition of man does the nature of things come into actual existence. If therefore it is required that man should not add anything to the things of the senses through his higher cognition, but should express only what already lies in them in the outside world, then this simply means renouncing all higher cognition.—From the fact that, as regards his sensory life, man is a thing among things, and that he only attains higher cognition when as a sensory being he himself accomplishes his transformation into a higher being, from this it follows that he can never replace the one cognition by the other. Rather, his spiritual life consists of a perpetual moving to and fro between the two poles of cognition, between *knowing* and *seeing*. If he shuts himself off from seeing, he forgoes the nature of things; if he were to shut himself off from sensory knowing, he would deprive himself of the things whose nature he wants to understand.—The same things reveal themselves to the lower understanding and to the higher seeing, only they do this at one time with regard to their external appearance, at the other time with regard to their inner essence.—Thus it is not due to things themselves that at a certain stage they appear only as external objects; rather it is due to the fact that man must first transform himself to the point where he can reach the stage at which things cease to be external.

It is only with these considerations in mind that certain views natural science elaborated in the nineteenth century appear in their proper light. The adherents of these views say to themselves: We hear, see, and touch the things of the material world through the senses. The eye, for instance, communicates to us a phenomenon of light, a color. We say that a body emits red light when, by the mediation of our eye, we have the sensation "red." But the eye gives us this sensation in other cases too. If it is struck or pressed, if an electric current passes through the head, the eye has a sensation of light. Hence in those instances also in which we have the sensation that a body emits light of a certain color, something may be occurring in that body which does not have any resemblance to color. No matter what is occurring in outside space, as long as this process is suitable for making an impression upon the eye, a sensation of color arises in me. What we perceive arises in us because we have organs that are constituted in a certain way. What goes on in outside space remains outside of us; we know only the effects which external processes bring forth in us. Hermann Helmholtz (1821-1894) has given

expression to this idea in a clearly defined way. "Our perceptions are effects produced in our organs by external
causes, and the way such an effect manifests itself is of
course substantially dependent on the kind of apparatus
acted upon. Insofar as the quality of our perception gives
us information about the characteristics of the external
influence by which it is caused, it can be considered as a
sign of the latter, but not as a *likeness* of it. For of an image one requires some kind of similarity to the object
represented: of a statue, similarity of form; of a drawing,
similarity of the perspective projection in the field of view;
of a painting, in addition to this, similarity of colors. But
a sign need not have any kind of resemblance to that of
which it is a sign. The relationship between the two is
limited to this, that the same object, exercising its influence under the same circumstances, calls forth the same
sign, and that therefore unlike signs always correspond to
unlike influences. . . . If in ripening berries of a certain
variety develop both a red pigment and sugar, then red
color and sweet taste will always be found together in our
perception of berries of this kind." (cf. Helmholtz: *Die
Tatsachen der Wahrnehmung,* The Facts of Perception,
p. 12 f.) I have characterized this way of thinking in detail
in my *Philosophie der Freiheit,* Philosophy of Spiritual
Activity, and in my *Rätsel der Philosophie,* Riddles of
Philosophy, 1918.—Let us now follow step by step the
train of thought which is adopted in this view. A process
is assumed in outside space. It produces an effect upon
my sensory organ; my nervous system transmits to my
brain the impression produced. Another process is effected

there. I now perceive "red." Now it is said: The perception of "red" is thus not outside; it is in me. All our perceptions are only *signs* of external processes, the real character of which we know nothing. We live and act among our perceptions, and know nothing about their origin. In line with this way of thinking one can also say: If we had no eye there would be no color; nothing would then transform the external process, which is unknown to us, into the perception "red." For many this train of thought is something seductive. Nevertheless it rests upon a complete misinterpretation of the facts under consideration. (If many contemporary natural scientists and philosophers were not deluded to a truly monstrous degree by this train of thought, one would not have to talk about it so much. But this delusion has in fact vitiated contemporary thinking in many respects.) Since man is a thing among things, it is of course necessary that things should make an impression upon him if he is to find out anything about them. A process outside of man must give rise to a process in man if the phenomenon "red" is to appear in the field of vision. One must only ask, What is outside, what inside? Outside is a process which takes place in space and time. But inside doubtless is a similar process. Such a process exists in the eye and communicates itself to the brain when I perceive "red." I cannot directly perceive the process which is "inside," any more than I can immediately perceive the wave motion "outside," which physicists consider corresponds to the color "red." But it is only in this sense that I can speak of an "outside" and an "inside." Only on the level of *sensory per-*

ception does the contrast between "outside" and "inside"
have any validity. This perception leads me to assume a
spatial-temporal process "outside," although I cannot perceive it *directly*. And, further, the same perception leads
me to assume such a process within me, although I cannot
perceive it directly either. But, after all, I also assume
spatial-temporal processes in ordinary life which I cannot
directly perceive.   For example, I hear a piano being
played in the next room. Therefore I assume that a human
being with spatial dimensions sits at the piano and plays.
And my way of representing things to myself is no different when I speak of processes *within* me and *outside* of
me. I assume that these processes have characteristics analogous to those of the processes which fall within the
domain of my senses, only that, for certain reasons, they
are not accessible to my direct observation. If I were
to deny to these processes all those qualities my senses
show me in the realm of the spatial and the temporal, I
would in truth be imagining something like the famous
knife without a handle of which the blade is missing.
Thus I can only say that "outside" occur spatial-temporal
processes, and that they cause spatial-temporal processes
"inside." Both are necessary if "red" is to appear in my
field of vision. Insofar as it is not spatial-temporal I shall
look for this red in vain, no matter whether I look for it
"outside" or "inside." The natural scientists and philosophers who cannot find it "outside" should not attempt to
look for it "inside" either. It is not "inside" in the same
sense in which it is not "outside." To declare that the entire content of what the world of the senses presents to us

is an inner world of perceptions, and to look for something "external" corresponding to it, is an impossible idea. Therefore we cannot say that "red," "sweet," "hot," etc. are *signs* which as such, are only caused to arise in us and to which something quite different on the "outside" corresponds. For what is really caused *in us* as the effect of an external process is something quite different from what appears in the field of our perceptions. If one wants to call what is *in us* signs, then one can say: These signs appear within our organism in order to communicate perceptions to us which, as such, in their immediacy are neither inside nor outside us, but rather belong to that common world of which my "external world" and my "interior world" are only parts. It is true that in order to be able to grasp this common world I must raise myself to that higher level of cognition for which an "inside" and an "outside" no longer exist. (I am well aware that people who rely on the gospel that "our entire world of experience" is made up of sensations of unknown origin will look down haughtily upon this exposition, in somewhat the same way as Dr. Erich Adikes in his work, *Kant contra Haeckel* says condescendingly: "For the time being, people like Haeckel and thousands of his kind philosophize merrily on, without worrying about any theory of cognition or about critical introspection." Such gentlemen of course have no suspicion of how paltry *their* theories of cognition are. They suspect a lack of critical introspection only in others. We shall not begrudge them their "wisdom.")

It is just on the point under consideration here that

Nicolas of Cusa has excellent ideas. His keeping the lower and the higher cognition clearly separated from each other permits him on the one hand to gain a full insight into the fact that as a sensory being man can have *within himself* only processes which must, as effects, be unlike the corresponding *external* processes; on the other hand, it preserves him from confusing the inner processes with the facts which appear in our field of perception and which, in their immediacy, are neither outside nor inside, but are elevated above this contrast.—Nicolas was "prevented by his priestly cloth" from following without reservations the path which this insight indicated to him. We see him making a good beginning with the advance from "knowing" to "not-knowing." But at the same time we must observe that in the field of "not-knowing" he has nothing to show except the theological teachings which are offered to us by the Scholastics also. It is true that he knows how to develop this theological content in an ingenious manner. On providence, Christ, the creation of the world, man's redemption, the moral life, he presents teachings which are altogether in line with dogmatic Christianity. It would have been in keeping with his spiritual direction to say: I have confidence that human nature, having immersed itself in the sciences of things on all sides, is able from within itself to transform this "knowing" into a "not-knowing," hence that the highest cognition brings satisfaction. Then he would not have accepted, as he has, the traditional ideas of soul, immortality, redemption, God, creation, the Trinity, etc., but would have upheld those which he himself had found.—But Nicolas, personally was so penetrated with the concepts of Christianity that he could well believe he was awakening his own proper "not-knowing" within himself, while he was only putting forth the traditional views in which he had been educated.— However it must be considered that he was standing before a fateful abyss in human spiritual life. He was a *scientific* man. And science at first removes man from the innocent concord in which he exists with the world as long as the conduct of his life is a purely naïve one. In such a conduct of life man dimly feels his connection with the totality of the universe. He is a being like others, integrated into the chain of natural effects. With knowledge he separates himself from this whole. He creates a spiritual world within himself. With it he confronts nature in solitude. He has become richer, but this wealth is a burden which he bears with difficulty. For at first it weighs upon him alone. He must find the way back to nature through his own resources. He must understand that now he himself must integrate his wealth into the chain of universal effects, as nature herself had integrated his poverty before. It is here that all the evil demons lie in wait for man. His strength can easily fail. Instead of accomplishing the integration himself, when this occurs, he will take refuge in a revelation from the outside, which again delivers him from his solitude, and leads the knowledge he feels to be a burden back into the primordial origin of existence, the Divinity. He will think, as did Nicolas of Cusa, that he is walking his own road, while in reality he will only find the one his spiritual development has shown him. Now there are three roads—in the main—upon which one can walk when one arrives where Nicolas had arrived: one is *positive faith,* which comes to us from outside; the second is *despair:* one stands alone with one's burden and feels all existence tottering with oneself; the third road is the development of man's own deepest faculties. *Confidence* in the world must be one leader along this third road. *Courage* to follow this confidence, no matter where it leads, must be the other[1].

---

[1] See Addendum III.

AGRIPPA OF NETTESHEIM AND
THEOPHRASTUS PARACELSUS

THE ROAD WHICH is indicated by the way of thinking of Nicolas of Cusa was walked by Heinrich Cornelius Agrippa of Nettesheim (1487-1535) and Theophrastus Paracelsus (1493-1541). They immerse themselves in nature and, as comprehensively as possible, seek to explore its laws with all the means their period makes available to them. In this knowledge of nature they see at the same time the true foundation for all higher cognition. They themselves seek to develop the latter out of natural science by letting science be reborn in the spirit.

Agrippa of Nettesheim led an eventful life. He was descended from a noble family and was born in Cologne. He studied medicine and jurisprudence at an early age and sought to inform himself about natural phenomena in the way customary at the time in certain circles and societies, or by contact with a number of scholars who carefully kept secret whatever insights they gained into nature. With such purposes he repeatedly went to Paris, to Italy, and to England, and he also visited the famous Abbot Trithemius of Sponheim in Würzburg. He taught in scientific institutions at various times and here and there entered the services of rich and noble personages, at whose disposal he placed his talents as a statesman and scientist. If his biographers describe the services he rendered as not always above reproach, if it is said that he acquired money under the pretext of being adept in secret arts, and of securing various advantages to people by means of these arts, this is counterbalanced by his unmistakable and ceaseless urge to acquire the entire learning of his time honestly and to make this learning deeper in the spirit of a higher cognition of the world. In him distinctly appears the endeavor to achieve a clear position with regard to natural science on the one hand, with regard to higher cognition on the other. Such a position is attained only by one who has an insight into the ways by which one reaches the one and the other cognition. Just as it is true that at last natural science must be raised into the region of the spirit if it is to lead into higher cognition, so it is true that it must at first remain in the field proper to it if it is to provide the right foundation for a higher level. The "spirit in nature" exists only for the spirit. As certainly as nature is in this sense spiritual, as certain is it that nothing perceived in nature by bodily organs is immediately spiritual. Nothing spiritual can appear to my eye as being spiritual. I must *not* seek the spirit as such in nature. I do this when I interpret a process of the external world in an immediately spiritual way: when, for instance, I ascribe to plants a soul which is only distantly analogous to the human soul. I also do this when I ascribe a spatial or temporal existence to the spirit or the soul itself; when, for instance, I say of the eternal human soul that it lives in time without the body, but still in the manner of a body, rather than as pure spirit. Or when I even believe that the spirit of a deceased person can show itself in some kind of sensorily perceptible manifestations. Spiritualism, which commits this error, thereby only shows that it has not penetrated to the true conception of the spirit, but wants to see the spirit directly in something grossly sensory. It fails to understand the nature of the sensory as well as that of the spirit. It deprives of spirit the ordinary sensory phenomena, which take place hour by hour before our eyes, in order to consider something rare, surprising, unusual as spirit in a direct sense. It does not understand that for one who is capable of seeing the spirit, what lives as "spirit in nature" reveals itself, for instance, in the collision of two elastic spheres, and not only in processes which arē striking because of their rarity and cannot be immediately grasped in their natural context. In addition, the spiritualist draws the spirit down into a lower sphere. Instead of explaining something that takes place in space and that he perceives with the senses by means of forces and beings which in turn are only spatial and sensorily perceptible, he has recourse to "spirits," which he thus equates completely with the sensorily perceptible. Such a way of thinking is based on a lack of capacity for spiritual comprehension. One is not capable of looking at the spiritual in a spiritual manner, therefore with mere sensory beings one satisfies one's need for the presence of the spirit. To such people the spirit does not show any spirit; therefore they seek it with the senses. As they see clouds sailing through the air, so they also want to see spirits hurrying along.

Agrippa of Nettesheim fights for a true natural science, which does not attempt to explain the phenomena of nature by spiritual beings which haunt the world of the senses, but sees in nature *only* the natural, in the spirit only the spiritual.—One would of course completely misunderstand Agrippa if one were to compare *his* natural science with that of later centuries, which has altogether different data at its disposal. In such a comparison it might easily appear that he still refers what is due only to natural causes, or based on erroneous data, to the direct action of spirits. Moritz Carriere does him this injustice when he says—although not with ill will—, "Agrippa gives a long list of the things which belong to the sun, the moon, the planets, or the fixed stars, and receive their influences; for instance, related to the sun are fire, blood, laurel, gold, chrysolite; they bestow the gift of the sun: courage, serenity, light. . . . The animals have a sense of nature which, more exalted than human reason, approaches the spirit of prophecy. . . . Men can be enjoined to love and hate, to sickness and health. Thus one puts a spell upon thieves that enjoins them from stealing somewhere, upon merchants so that they cannot trade, ships and mills so that they cannot move, lightning so that it cannot strike. This is done with potions, salves, images, rings, charms; the blood of hyenas or basilisks is suitable for this purpose,—*one is reminded of Shakespeare's witches' cauldron.*" No, one is not reminded of it, if one understands Agrippa aright. He did of course believe in things which were considered to be indubitable in his time. But we do this today also with regard to what is nowadays considered "factual." Or is one to believe that future centuries also will not throw much of what we set up as indubitable facts into the store-room of "blind" superstition? It is true that I am convinced that there is a real progress in man's knowledge of facts. When the "fact" that the earth is round had once been discovered, all earlier suppositions were banished into the realm of "superstition." Thus it is with certain truths of astronomy, of biology, etc. The doctrine of natural descent, in comparison with all earlier "hypotheses of creation," represents a progress similar to the insight that the earth is round compared to all previous suppositions concerning its shape. Nevertheless I am aware that there is many a "fact" in our learned scientific works and treatises which will no more appear as fact to future centuries than does much of what is maintained by Agrippa and Paracelsus to us today. It is not a matter of what they considered to be a "fact," but of the spirit in which they interpreted these facts.—In Agrippa's time one found, it is true, little comprehension of the "natural magic" which he advocated, and which seeks in nature the natural, and the spiritual only in the spirit; men clung to the "supernatural magic" which seeks the spiritual in the realm of the sensory, and against which Agrippa fought. This is why the Abbot Trithemius of Sponheim advised him to communicate his views as a secret doctrine only to a few chosen ones, who were able to rise to a similar conception of nature and spirit, for "one gives only hay to oxen and not sugar, as to songbirds." It is perhaps to this abbot that Agrippa himself owes the right point of view. In his *Steganographie,* Steganography, Trithemius has written a work in which he treats, with the most veiled irony, the way of thinking which confounds nature with the spirit. In this book he appears to speak entirely of supernatural phenomena. One who reads it as it stands must believe that the author is speaking of the conjuring of spirits, of the flying of spirits through the air, etc. But if one omits certain words and letters of the text there remain—as Wolfgang Ernst Heidel showed in the year 1676—letters which, when assembled into words, describe purely natural phenomena. (In one case for instance, in a formula of incantation, one must completely omit the first and the last word, and then cross out the second, fourth, sixth, etc. of those remaining. In the remaining words one must again cross out the first, third, fifth, etc. letter. What remains, one then assembles into words, and the formula of incantation is transformed into a communication of a purely natural content.)

How difficult it was for Agrippa to work his way out of the prejudices of his time and to raise himself to a pure conception, is proven by the fact that he did not let his *Philosophia occulta,* Secret Philosophy, appear until the year 1531, although it had been composed as early as 1510, because he considered it to be immature. Further evidence of this is given in his work, *De vanitate scientiarum,* Of the Vanity of the Sciences, where he speaks with bitterness about the scientific and general activity of his time. There he says quite plainly that only with difficulty has he liberated himself from the delusion of those who see in external events direct spiritual processes, in external facts prophetic hints about the future, etc. Agrippa proceeds to the higher cognition in three stages. At the first stage he deals with the world as it is presented to the senses, with its substances, and its physical, chemical, and other forces. Insofar as it is viewed at this stage he calls nature elemental. At the second stage one regards the world as a whole in its natural connections, in the way it arranges everything belonging to it according to measurements, number, weight, harmony, etc. The first stage brings those things together which are in close proximity to each other. It seeks the causes of a phenomenon which lie in its immediate environment. The second stage looks at a single phenomenon in connection with the whole universe. It carries out the idea that each thing is under the influence of all the remaining things of the universal whole. This universal whole appears to it as a great harmony, of which every separate entity is a part. The world, seen from this point of view, is designated by Agrippa as the astral or celestial one. The third stage of cognition is that where the spirit, through immersion in itself, looks directly upon the spiritual, the primordial essence of the world. Here Agrippa speaks of the spiritual-soul world.

The views which Agrippa developed about the world and man's relationship to it we encounter in a similar, but more complete form in Theophrastus Paracelsus. They are therefore better considered in connection with the latter.

Paracelsus characterizes himself when he writes under his portrait, "No one who can stand alone by himself should be the servant of another." His whole position with regard to cognition is given in these words. Everywhere he himself wants to go back to the foundations of natural science in order to ascend, through his own powers, to the highest regions of cognition. As a physician he does not simply want to accept, like his contemporaries, what the old investigators who at the time were considered authorities, as for instance Galen or Avicenna, had affirmed in times gone by; he himself wants to read directly in the *book of nature*. "The physician must pass through the examination of nature, which is the world, and all its causation. And what nature teaches him he must commend to his wisdom, not seeking anything in his wisdom, but only in the light of nature." He does not recoil from anything in order to become acquainted with nature and its manifestations from all sides. For this purpose he travels to Sweden, Hungary, Spain, Portugal, and the Orient. He can say of himself, "I have pursued the art in danger of my life and have not been ashamed to learn from strollers, hangmen, and barbers. My teachings have been tested more severely than silver in poverty, anxiety, wars, and perils." What has been handed down from old authorities has no value for him, for he believes that he can only attain the right conception if he himself experiences the ascent from natural science to the highest cognition. This experiencing in his own person puts the proud words in his mouth, "One who wants to pursue the truth must come into my realm. . . . After me, not I after you, Avicenna, Rhases, Galen, Mesur! After me, and I not after you, you of Paris, you of Montpellier, you of Swabia, you

of Meissen, you of Cologne, you of Vienna, and whatever
lies on the Danube and the river Rhine, you islands in the
sea, you Italy, you Dalmatia, you Athens, you Greek, you
Arab, you Israelite; after me, and I not after you! Mine
is the realm!"—It is easy to misjudge Paracelsus because
of his rough exterior, which sometimes hides deep serious-
ness behind jest. He himself says, "Nature has not made
me subtle, nor have I been raised on figs and white bread,
but rather on cheese, milk, and oat bread, and therefore
I may well be uncivil to the hyperclean and the super-
fine; for those who were brought up in soft clothes and we,
who were brought up among fir-cones, do not understand
each other well. Thus I must seem rough, though to myself I appear gracious. How can I not be strange for one
who has never gone wandering in the sun?"

Goethe has described the relationship of man to nature (in his book on Winkelmann) in the following beautiful sentences: "When the healthy nature of man acts as
a whole, when he feels himself to be in the world as in a
great, beautiful, noble, and valued whole, when harmonious ease affords him a pure and free delight, then the
universe, if it could experience itself, would exult, *as having attained its goal,* and *admire the climax of its own becoming and essence."* Paracelsus is deeply penetrated with
a sentiment like the one that expresses itself in such sentences. Out of this sentiment the mystery of man shapes
itself for him. Let us see how this happens, in Paracelsus'
sense. At first the road which nature has taken in order to
bring forth its highest achievement is hidden from the
human powers of comprehension. It has attained this

climax; but this climax does not say, I feel myself to be the whole of nature; this climax says, I feel myself to be this single man. What in reality is an act of the whole world feels itself to be a single, solitary being, standing by itself. Indeed, this is the true nature of man, that he must feel himself as being something other than what, in the final analysis, he is. And if this is a contradiction, then man can be called a contradiction come to life. Man in his own way is the world. His harmony with the world he regards as a duality. He is the same as the world is, but he is this as a repetition, as a separate being. This is the contrast which Paracelsus perceives as microcosm (man) and macrocosm (universe). For him man is the world in little. What causes man to regard his relationship with the world in this way is his spirit. This spirit appears to be bound to a single being, to a single organism. By its whole nature, this organism belongs to the great chain of the universe. It is a link in it, and has its existence only in connection with all the others. The spirit, however, appears to be an outcome of this single organism. At first it sees itself as connected only with this organism. It tears this organism loose from the native soil out of which it grew. For Paracelsus a deep connection between man and the entire universe thus lies hidden in the natural foundation of existence, a connection which is obscured by the presence of the spirit. For us humans, the spirit, which leads us to higher cognition by communicating knowledge to us and by causing this knowledge to be reborn on a higher level, has at first the effect of obscuring for us our own connection with the universe. For Paracelsus human nature thus at first falls into three parts: into our sensory-corporeal nature, our organism, which appears to us as a natural being among other natural beings, and which is just like all other natural beings; into our hidden nature, which is a link in the chain of the whole world, which thus is not enclosed within our organism, but sends out and receives influences to and from the whole universe; and into the highest nature, our spirit, which lives its life only in a spiritual manner. The first part of human nature Paracelsus calls the *elemental body;* the second the ethereal-celestial or *"astral body;"* the third part he calls *soul.*—In the "astral" phenomena Paracelsus thus sees an intermediate level between the purely corporeal phenomena and the true phenomena of the soul. They will become visible when the spirit, which obscures the natural foundation of our existence, ceases its activity. We can see the simplest manifestation of this realm in the world of dreams. The images which flit through our dreams, with their peculiar, significant connection with events in our environment and with our own internal states, are products of our natural foundation which are obscured by the brighter light of the soul. When a chair collapses near my bed, and I dream a whole drama, which ends with a shot fired in a duel, or when I have palpitations of the heart, and dream of a seething stove, then meaningful and significant natural manifestations are appearing which reveal a life lying between the purely organic functions and the thinking processes taking place in the bright consciousness of the spirit. With this realm are connected all the phenomena which belong to the field of hypnotism and of suggestion. In suggestion we can see an acting of man on man, which points to an interrelationship between beings in nature that is obscured by the higher activity of the spirit. In this connection it becomes possible to understand what Paracelsus interprets as an "astral body." It is the sum of the natural influences to which we are exposed or can be exposed through special circumstances, which emanate from us without involving our soul, and which nevertheless do not fall under the concept of purely physical phenomena. That in this field Paracelsus enumerates facts which we doubt today, has no importance when looked at from the point of view I have already adduced above (cf. p. 192).—On the basis of such views of human nature Paracelsus divides the latter into seven parts. They are the same as we find in the teachings of the ancient Egyptians, among the Neoplatonists, and in the Cabala. Man is first of all a physical-corporeal being; hence he is subject to the same laws to which *every* body is subject. In this sense he is thus a purely *elemental* body. The purely corporeal-physical laws combine in the *organic* life process. Paracelsus designates the organic laws as "Archaeus" or "Spiritus vitae;" the organic raises itself to spiritlike manifestations which are not yet spirit. These are the *"astral"* manifestations. From the "astral" processes emerge the functions of the *"animal spirit."* Man is a sense being. He combines his sensory impressions in a rational manner by means of his reason. Thus the *"rational soul"* awakens in him. He immerses himself in his own spiritual products; he learns to recognize the spirit as spirit. Therewith he has raised himself to the level of the *"spiritual soul."*

At last he understands that in this spiritual soul he experiences the deepest stratum of the universal existence; the spiritual soul ceases to be an individual, separate one. The insight takes place of which Eckhart spoke when he felt that it was no longer *he himself* who spoke in him, but the primordial essence. Now that condition prevails in which the universal spirit regards itself in man. Paracelsus has expressed the feeling aroused by this condition in the simple words: "And this which you must consider is something great: there is nothing in Heaven and on earth which is not in man. And *God,* who is in Heaven, is in man."—It is nothing but facts of external and internal experience that Paracelsus wants to express with these seven fundamental parts of human nature. That what for human experience falls into a plurality of seven parts is in higher reality a unity is not thereby brought into question. The higher cognition exists precis to show the unity in everything which in his immediate experience appears to man as a plurality because of his corporeal and spiritual organization. On the level of the highest cognition Paracelsus strives to fuse the living, uniform, primordial essence of the world with his spirit. But he knows that man can only know nature in its spirituality if he enters into immediate intercourse with it. Man does not understand nature by peopling it, on his own, with arbitrarily assumed spiritual entities, but by accepting and valuing it as it is as nature. Paracelsus therefore does not seek God or the spirit *in* nature; but for him nature, as it presents itself to his eye, is immediately *divine.* Must one first attribute to the plant a soul like the human soul in order to find the spiritual? Therefore Paracelsus explains the development of things, insofar as this is possible with the scientific resources of his time, entirely in such a way that he regards this development as a sensory process of nature. He lets everything arise out of the primordial matter, the primordial water (Yliaster). And he regards as a further process of nature the separation of the primordial matter (which he also calls the great limbus) into the four elements, water, earth, fire, and air. When he says that the "divine word" called forth the plurality of beings from the primordial matter, this is only to be understood in somewhat the same manner as the relationship of force to matter is to be understood in modern natural science. A "spirit" in the real sense is not yet present on this level. This "spirit" is not an actual cause of the natural process, but an actual result of this process. This spirit does not create nature, but develops out of it. Many words of Paracelsus could be interpreted in the opposite sense. Thus, for instance, he says: "There is nothing corporeal that does not carry a living spirit hidden within it. And not only *that* has life which stirs and moves, such as men, animals, the worms in the earth, the birds in the sky, and the fish in the water, but all corporeal and substantial things." But with such sayings Paracelsus only wants to warn against the superficial view of nature which thinks that it can exhaust the nature of a thing with a few "rammed-in" concepts (to use Goethe's apt expression). He does not want to inject an invented nature into things, but rather to set all the faculties of man in motion in order to bring forth what actually lies within a thing.—It is important not to let oneself be misled by the fact that

Paracelsus expresses himself in the spirit of his time. Rather, one should try to understand what he has in mind when, looking upon nature, he sets forth his ideas in the forms of expression of his time. For instance, he ascribes to man a twofold flesh, that is, a twofold corporeal constitution. "The flesh must therefore he understood to be of two kinds, namely, the flesh whose origin is in Adam, and the flesh which is not from Adam. The flesh that is from Adam is a coarse flesh, for it is earthly and nothing but flesh, and is to be bound and grasped like wood and stone. The other flesh is not from Adam; it is a subtle flesh and is not to be bound or grasped, for it is not made of earth." What is the flesh that is from Adam? It is all that has come down to man through his *natural* development, which he has therefore *inherited*. To this is added what in the course of time man has *acquired* for himself in intercourse with his environment. The modern scientific concepts of *inherited* characteristics and of characteristics *acquired through adaptation* emerge from the above-mentioned thought of Paracelsus. The "subtler flesh," which makes man capable of spiritual activities, has not been in man from the beginning. He was "coarse flesh" like the animals, a flesh that "is to be bound and grasped like wood and stone." In the scientific sense the soul is therefore also an *acquired* characteristic of the "coarse flesh." What the natural scientist of the nineteenth century has in mind when he speaks of the inheritances from the animal world, is what Paracelsus means when he uses the expression about "the flesh whose origin is in Adam." These remarks, of course, are not intended to obliterate the difference

which exists between a natural scientist of the sixteenth
and one of the nineteenth century. After all, it was only
the latter century which was capable of seeing, in the
full scientific sense, the forms of living organisms in such
a connection that their natural relationship and their
actual descent as far as man became evident. Science sees
only a natural process where Linné in the eighteenth century still saw a spiritual process, which he characterized in
the following words: "There are as many species of living
organisms as there were, in principle, forms that were
created." While Linné thus had to transfer the spirit into
the spatial world and assign to it the task of producing
spiritually, of "creating" the forms of life, the natural
science of the nineteenth century could ascribe to nature
what is nature's and to the spirit what is the spirit's. Nature itself is assigned the task of explaining its creations,
and the spirit can immerse itself into itself where it alone
is to be found, within man.—But while in a certain sense
Paracelsus thinks quite in the spirit of his time, yet just
with regard to the idea of *development,* of *becoming,* he
has grasped the relationship of man to nature in a profound manner. In the primordial essence of the world he
did not see something which in some way exists as something finished, but he grasped the divine in its becoming.
Hence he could really ascribe a self-creating activity to
man. If the divine primordial essence exists, once and for
all a true creating by man is out of the question. Then it
is not man, who lives in time, who creates, but God, Who
is eternal. For Him there is only an eternal becoming, and
man is a link in this eternal becoming. That which man

forms did not previously exist in any way. What man creates, as he creates it, is an original creation. If it is to be called divine, this can only be in the sense in which it exists as a human creation. Therefore in the building of the universe Paracelsus can assign to man a role which makes him a co-architect in this creation. The divine primordial essence *without* man is not what it is *with* man. "For nature brings forth nothing into the light of day which is complete as it stands; rather, man must complete it." This self-creating activity of man in the building of nature, Paracelsus calls alchemy. "This completion is alchemy. Thus the alchemist is the baker when he bakes the bread, the vintager when he makes the wine, the weaver when he makes the cloth." Paracelsus wants to be an alchemist in his field, as a physician. "Therefore I may well write so much here concerning alchemy, so that you can know it well and learn what it is and how it is to be understood, nor be vexed that it is to bring you neither gold nor silver. Rather see that the arcana (remedies) are revealed to you. . . . The third pillar of medicine is alchemy, for the preparation of remedies cannot take place without it, *because nature cannot be put to use without art.*"

Thus Paracelsus' eyes are directed in the strictest sense upon nature, in order to discover from nature itself what it has to say about its products. He wants to investigate the laws of chemistry in order to work as an alchemist in his sense. He considers all bodies to be composed of three basic substances, namely, of salt, sulphur, and mercury. What he so designates of course does not correspond to what later chemistry designates by this name, any more than what Paracelsus considers to be a basic substance is one in the sense of later chemistry. Different things are designated by the same names at different times. What the ancients called the four elements, earth, water, air, and fire, we still have. We call these four "elements" no longer "elements" but states of aggregation, for which we have the designations: solid, liquid, aeriform, etheriform. Earth, for instance, for the ancients was not earth but the "solid." The three basic substances of Paracelsus we can also recognize in contemporary concepts, but not under the homonymous contemporary names. For Paracelsus, solution in a liquid and combustion are the two important chemical processes of which he makes use. If a body is dissolved or burned it is decomposed into its parts. Something remains as residue; something is dissolved or burns. For him the residue is salt-like, the soluble (liquid), mercury-like; the combustible he calls sulphurous.

One who does not look beyond such natural processes may be left cold by them as by things of a material and prosaic nature; one who at all costs wants to grasp the spirit with the senses will people these processes with all kinds of spiritual beings. But like Paracelsus, one who knows how to look at such processes in connection with the universe, which reveals its secret within man, accepts these processes as they present themselves to the senses; he does not first reinterpret them; for as the natural processes stand before us in their sensory reality, in their own way they reveal the mystery of existence. What through this sensory reality these processes reveal out of the soul of man, occupies a higher position for one who strives for the light of higher cognition than do all the supernatural miracles concerning their so-called "spirit" which man can devise or have revealed to him. There is no "spirit of nature" which can utter more exalted truths than the great works of nature themselves, when our soul unites itself with this nature in friendship, and, in familiar intercourse, hearkens to the revelations of its secrets. Such a friendship with nature, Paracelsus sought.

VALENTIN WEIGEL AND JACOB BOEHME

PARACELSUS was primarily concerned with developing ideas about nature that breathe the spirit of the higher cognition he advocated. A kindred thinker who applied the same way of thinking to man's own nature in particular is Valentin Weigel (1533-1588). He grew out of Protestant theology as Eckhart, Tauler, and Suso grew out of Catholic theology. He had precursors in Sebastian Frank and Caspar Schwenckfeldt. They emphasized the deepening of the inner life, in contrast to the church dogma with its attachment to an external creed. For them it is not the Jesus whom the Gospels preach who is of value, but the Christ who can be born in every man out of his deeper nature, and who is to be his deliverer from the lower life and his leader in the ascent to the ideal. Weigel quietly and modestly administered his incumbency in Zschopau. It is only from his posthumous writings printed in the seventeenth century that one discovers something about the significant ideas he had developed concerning the nature of man. (Of his writings we shall mention here: *Der güldene Griff, Alle Ding ohne Irrthumb zu erkennen,*

*vielen Hochgelährten unbekannt, und doch allen Men-
schen nothwendig zu wissen,* The Golden art of Knowing Everything without Error, unknown to Many of the
Learned, and yet Necessary for all Men to Know.—*Erkenne dich selber,* Know Thyself.—*Vom Ort der Welt,* Of
the Place of the World.) Weigel is anxious to come to a
clear idea of his relationship to the teachings of the Church.
This leads him to investigate the foundations of all cognition. Man can only decide whether he can know something through a creed if he understands *how* he knows.
Weigel takes his departure from the lowest kind of cognition. He asks himself, How do I apprehend a sensory thing
when it confronts me? From there he hopes to be able
to ascend to the point where he can give an account of
the highest cognition.—In sensory apprehension the instrument (sense organ) and the thing, the "counterpart,"
confront each other. "Since in natural perception there
must be two things, namely the object or counterpart,
which is to be perceived and seen by the eye, and the eye,
or the perceiver, which sees and perceives the object,
therefore, consider the question, Does the perception come
from the object into the eye, or does the judgment, and
the perception, flow from the eye into the object." (*Der
güldene Griff,* chap. 9) Now Weigel says to himself, If
the perception flowed from the counterpart (thing) into
the eye, then, of one and the same thing, the same complete perception would of necessity have to arise in all
eyes. But this is not the case; rather, everyone sees according to his eyes. Only the eyes, not the counterpart, can
be responsible for the fact that many different concep-

tions of one and the same thing are possible. In order to make the matter clear, Weigel compares seeing with reading. If the book did not exist of course I could not read it; but it could be there, and I would still not be able to read anything in it if I did not know the art of reading. Thus the book must be there, but of itself it cannot give me anything at all; everything that I read I must bring forth out of myself. That is also the nature of natural (sensory) perception. Color exists as a "counterpart;" but out of itself it cannot give the eye anything. On its own, the eye must perceive what color is. The color is no more in the eye than the content of the book is in the reader. If the content of the book were in the reader, he would not have to read it. Nevertheless, in reading, this content does not flow out of the book, but out of the reader. It is the same with the sensory object. What this sensory object is outside, does not flow into man from the outside, but rather from the inside.—On the basis of these ideas one could say, If all perception flows from man into the object, then one does not perceive what is in the object, but only what is in man himself. A detailed elaboration of this train of thought is presented in the views of Immanuel Kant (1724-1804). (I have shown the erroneous aspect of this train of thought in my book, *Philosophie der Freiheit*, Philosophy of Spiritual Activity. Here I must confine myself to saying that with this simple, straightforward way of thinking Valentin Weigel stands on a much higher level than Kant.)—Weigel says to himself, Although perception flows from man yet it is only the nature of the counterpart which emerges from the latter by way

of man. As it is the content of the book which I discover
by reading and not my own, so it is the color of the counterpart which I discover through the eye, not the color
which is in the eye, or in me. On his own path Weigel
thus comes to a conclusion which we have already encoun-
tered in the thinking of Nicolas of Cusa. In his way
Weigel has elucidated the nature of sensory perception for
himself. He has attained the conviction that everything
external things have to tell us can only flow out from
within ourselves. Man cannot remain passive if he wants to
perceive the things of the senses, and be content with letting them act upon him; he must be active, and bring this
perception out of *himself*. The counterpart alone awakens
the perception in the spirit. Man ascends to higher cognition when the spirit becomes its own object. In considering sensory perception, one can see that no cognition can
flow into man from the outside. Therefore the higher
cognition cannot come from the outside, but can only be
awakened within man. Hence there can be no external
revelation, but only an inner awakening. And as the external counterpart waits until man confronts it, in whom
it can express its nature, so must man wait, when he wants
to be his own counterpart, until the cognition of his nature is awakened in him. While in the sensory perception man must be active in order to present the counterpart with its nature, in the higher cognition he must remain passive, because now *he* is the counterpart. He must
receive his nature within himself. Because of this the
cognition of the spirit appears to him as an illumination
from on high. In contrast with the sensory perception,

Weigel therefore calls the higher cognition the "light of grace." This "light of grace" is in reality nothing but the self-cognition of the spirit in man, or the rebirth of knowledge on the higher level of seeing.—As Nicolas of Cusa, in pursuing his road from knowing to seeing, does not really let the knowledge acquired by him be reborn on a higher level, but is deceived into regarding the church creed, in which he had been educated, as this rebirth, so is this the case with Weigel too. He finds his way to the right road, and loses it again at the moment he enters upon it. One who wants to walk the road which Weigel indicates can regard the latter as a leader only up to its starting-point.

*

What we encounter in the works of the master shoemaker of Görlitz, Jacob Boehme (1575-1624), is like the jubilation of nature, which, at the peak of its development, admires its essence. Before us appears a man whose words have wings, woven out of the blissful feeling that he sees the knowledge in himself shining as higher wisdom. Jacob Boehme describes his condition as a devotion which only desires to be wisdom, and as a wisdom which desires to live in devotion alone: "When I wrestled and fought, with God's assistance, there arose a wondrous light in my soul which was altogether foreign to wild nature, and by which I first understood what God and man are, and what God has to do with man." Jacob Boehme no longer feels himself to be a separate personality which utters its insights; he feels himself to be an organ of the great universal spirit which speaks in him. The limits of his personality do not appear to him as limits of the spirit which speaks out of him. For him this spirit is omnipresent. He knows that "the sophist will censure him" when he speaks of the beginning of the world and of its creation, "since I was not there and did not see it myself. Let him be told that in the essence of my soul and body, when I was not yet the I, but Adam's essence, I was indeed there, and that I myself have forfeited my felicity in Adam." It is only in external similes that Boehme can intimate how the light broke forth within himself. When as a boy he once is on the summit of a mountain, above where great red stones seem to close the mountain off, he sees an open entrance, and in its depths a vessel containing gold. He is overcome with awe, and goes his way without touching the treasure. Later he is serving his apprenticeship with a shoemaker in Görlitz. A stranger walks into the store and asks for a pair of shoes. Boehme is not allowed to sell them to him in the master's absence. The stranger leaves, but after a while calls the apprentice outside and says to him, Jacob, you are little, but one day you will become an altogether different man, at whom the world will be filled with astonishment. At a more mature period of his life, Jacob Boehme sees the sunshine reflected in a burnished pewter vessel; the sight which confronts him seems to him to reveal a profound mystery. From the time he experiences this manifestation he believes himself to be in possession of the key to the mysterious language of nature.—He lives as a spiritual hermit, supporting himself modestly by his trade, and at the same time setting down, as if for his own memory, the notes which sound in him when he feels the spirit within himself. The zealotry of priestly fanaticism makes his life difficult. He wants to read only that scripture which the light within himself illuminates for him, but is pursued and tormented by those to whom only the external scripture, the rigid, dogmatic creed, is accessible.

Jacob Boehme is filled with a restlessness which impels him toward cognition, because a universal mystery lives in his soul. He feels himself to be immersed in a divine harmony with his spirit, but when he looks around him he sees disharmony everywhere in the divine works. To man belongs the light of wisdom, yet he is exposed to error; there lives in him the impulse toward the good, and yet the dissonance of evil can be heard throughout the course of human development. Nature is governed by great natural laws, and yet its harmony is disturbed by superfluities and by the wild struggle of the elements. How is the disharmony in the harmonious, universal whole to be understood? This question torments Jacob Boehme. It comes to occupy the center of his world of ideas. He wants to attain a conception of the universal whole which includes the inharmonious too. For how can a conception explain the world which leaves the existing inharmonious elements aside, unexplained? Disharmony must be explained through harmony, evil through good itself. In speaking of these things, let us limit ourselves to good and evil; in the latter, disharmony in the narrower sense finds its expression in human life. For this is what Jacob Boehme basically limits himself to. He can do this,

for to him nature and man appear as one essence. He
sees similar laws and processes in both. The non-functional is for him an evil in nature, just as the evil is for
him something non-functional in human destiny. Here
and there it is the same basic forces which are at work.
To one who has understood the origin of evil in man, the
origin of evil in nature is also plain.—How is it possible
for evil as well as for good to flow out of the same primordial essence? If one speaks in the spirit of Jacob Boehme,
one gives the following answer: The primordial essence
does not exist in itself alone. The diversity of the world
participates in this existence. As the human body does not
live its life as a single part, but as a multiplicity of parts,
so too does the primordial essence. And as human life is
poured into this multiplicity of parts, so is the primordial
essence poured into the diversity of the things of this
world. Just as it is true that the whole man has *one* life,
so is it true that each part has its own life. And it no more
contradicts the whole harmonious life of man that his
hand should turn against his own body and wound it,
than it is impossible that the things of the world, which
live the life of the primordial essence in their own way,
should turn against one another. Thus the primordial
life, in distributing itself over different lives, bestows upon
each life the capacity of turning itself against the whole.
It is not out of the good that the evil flows, but out of
the manner in which the good lives. As the light can only
shine when it penetrates the darkness, so the good can only
come to life when it permeates its opposite. Out of the
"abyss" of darkness shines the light; out of the "abyss" of

the indifferent, the good brings itself forth. And as in the shadow it is only brightness which requires a reference to light, while the darkness is felt to be self-evident, as something that weakens the light, so too in the world it is only the lawfulness in all things which is sought, and the evil, the non-functional, which is accepted as the self-evident. Hence, although for Jacob Boehme the primordial essence is the All, nothing in the world can be understood unless one keeps in sight both the primordial essence and its opposite. "The good has swallowed the evil or the repugnant into itself. . . . Every being has good and evil within itself; and in its development, having to decide between them, it becomes an opposition of qualities, since one of them seeks to overcome the other." It is therefore entirely in the spirit of Jacob Boehme to see both good and evil in every object and process of the world; but it is not in his spirit to seek the primordial essence without further ado in the mixture of the good with the evil. The primordial essence had to swallow the evil, but the evil is not a part of the primordial essence. Jacob Boehme seeks the primordial foundation of the world, but the world itself arose out of the abyss by means of the primordial foundation. "The external world is not God, and in eternity is not to be called God, but is only a being in which God reveals Himself. . . . When one says, God is everything, God is heaven and earth and also the external world, then this is true; for everything has its origin from Him and in Him. But what am I to do with such a saying that is not a religion?"—With this conception as a background, his ideas about the nature of the world developed in Jacob Boehme's spirit in such a way that he lets the lawful world arise out of the abyss in a succession of stages. This world is built up in seven natural forms. The primordial essence receives a form in dark acerbity, silently enclosed within itself and motionless. It is under the symbol of *salt* that Boehme conceives this acerbity. With such designations he leans upon Paracelsus, who has borrowed the names for the process of nature from the chemical processes (cf. p. 205 above). By swallowing its opposite, the first natural form takes on the shape of the second; the harsh and motionless takes on motion; energy and life enter into it. Mercury is the symbol for this second form. In the struggle of stillness with motion, of death with life, the third natural form (sulphur) appears. This life, with its internal struggle, is revealed to itself; henceforth it does not live in an external struggle of its parts; like a uniformly shining lightning, illuminating itself, it thrills through its own being (fire). This fourth natural form ascends to the fifth, the living struggle of the parts reposing within itself (water). On this level exists an inner acerbity and silence as on the first, only it is not an absolute quiet, a silence of the inner contrasts, but an inner movement of the contrasts. It is not the quiet which reposes within itself, but which has motion, which was kindled by the fiery lightning of the fourth stage. On the sixth level, the primordial essence itself becomes aware of itself as such an inner life; it perceives itself through sense organs. It is the living organisms, endowed with senses, which represent this natural form. Jacob Boehme calls it sound or resonance, and thus sets up the sensory impression of hearing as a symbol for sensory perception in general. The seventh natural form is the spirit elevating itself by virtue of its sensory perceptions (wisdom). It finds itself again as itself, as the primordial foundation, within the world which has grown out of the abyss and shaped itself out of harmonious and inharmonious elements. "The Holy Ghost brings the splendor of majesty into the entity in which the Divinity stands revealed."—With such conceptions Jacob Boehme seeks to fathom *that* world which, in accordance with the knowledge of his time, appears to him as the real one. For him facts are what the natural science of his time and the Bible regard as such. His way of thinking is one thing, his world of facts another. One can imagine the former as applied to a quite different factual knowledge. And thus there appears before our mind a Jacob Boehme who could also be living at the turn of the nineteenth to the twentieth century. Such a man would not penetrate with his thinking the biblical story of the Creation and the struggle of the angels with the devils, but rather Lyell's geological insights and the "natural history of creation" of Haeckel. One who penetrates to the *spirit* of Jacob Boehme's writings must come to this conviction.* (We shall mention the most important of these writings: *Die Morgenröthe im Aufgang,* The Coming of the Dawn. *Die drei Prinzipien göttlichen Wesens,* The Three Principles of the Divine Essence. *Vom dreifachen Leben des Menschen,* Of the Threefold Life of Man. *Das umgewandte Auge,* The Eye Turned

Upon Itself. *Signatura rerum oder von der Geburt und Bezeichnung aller Wesen, Signatura rerum* or of the birth and designation of all beings. *Mysterium magnum.*)

---

* This sentence must not be understood as meaning that the investigation of the Bible and of the spiritual world would be an aberration at the present time; what is meant is that a "Jacob Boehme of the nineteenth century" would be led by paths similar to those which led the one of the sixteenth century to the Bible, to the "natural history of creation." But from there he would press forward to the spiritual world.

GIORDANO BRUNO
AND ANGELUS SILESIUS

IN THE FIRST DECADE of the sixteenth century, at Castle
Heilsberg in Prussia, the scientific genius of Nicolas Copernicus (1473-1543) is erecting an edifice of ideas which will
compel men of succeeding epochs to look up to the starry
heavens with conceptions different from those which their
ancestors had in antiquity and in the Middle Ages. To
the latter, the earth was a dwelling-place resting at the center of the universe. The stars, on the other hand, were for
them entities of a perfect nature, the movement of which
proceeded in circles because the circle is the image of
perfection.—In what the stars showed to the human senses
one saw something belonging directly to the soul or the
spirit. The objects and events of the earth spoke one language to man; another language was spoken by the shining stars which, in the pure ether beyond the moon,
seemed to be a spiritual being that filled space. Nicolas
of Cusa had already formed different ideas. Through
Copernicus the earth became for man a fellow creation
among the other heavenly bodies, a star that moved like

others. Everything in the earth which appeared to man as being different, he could now attribute only to the fact that it is his dwelling-place. He was compelled to stop thinking in different ways about the phenomena of this earth and about those of the remainder of the universe. His sensory world had expanded into furthest space. What reached his eye from the ether he now had to accept as belonging to the sensory world, like the things of the earth. He could no longer seek the spirit in the ether in a sensory fashion.

All who henceforth strove for higher cognition had to come to terms with this expanded sensory world. In earlier centuries, the meditating spirit of man had stood before another world of facts. Now it was given a new task. It was no longer the things of this earth alone which could express their nature out of the interior of man. This interior had to enfold the spirit of a sensory world, which fills the spatial universe everywhere in an identical fashion.—It was such a task that confronted the thinker from Nola, Philotheo Giordano Bruno (1548-1600). The senses have conquered the spatial universe for themselves; now the spirit is no longer to be found in space. Thus man was directed from outside to seek the spirit henceforth only where, on the basis of deep inner experiences, it had been sought by the glorious thinkers who have been discussed in the preceding expositions. These thinkers draw out of themselves a conception of the world to which men later are to be compelled by a more advanced natural science. The sun of ideas which later is to fall upon a new conception of nature, with them is still beneath the hori-

222 Mysticism at the Dawn of the Modern Age

zon, but its light already appears as a dawn in a time when men's thoughts about nature are still enveloped in the darkness of night.—For the purposes of science the sixteenth century gave the heavens to that world of the senses to which they rightfully belong; up to the end of the nineteenth century this science had progressed so far that from among the phenomena of plant, animal, and human life also it could give to the world of sensory facts what belongs to it. Neither up in the ether nor in the development of living organisms can this science henceforth look for anything but factual-sensory processes. As the thinker of the sixteenth century had to say: The earth is a star among stars, subject to the same laws as other stars, so the thinker of the nineteenth century must say, "Whatever his origin and his future may be, for anthropology man is only a mammal; specifically he is that mammal whose organization, needs, and diseases are the most complicated, and whose brain with its wonderful capacity, has reached the highest degree of development." (Paul Topinard, *Anthropologie*, Anthropology, Leipzig, 1888, p. 528.)—On the basis of this point of view attained by science, a confusion of the spiritual with the sensory can no longer take place, if man understands himself aright. An advanced science makes it impossible to seek in nature a spirit conceived along the lines of the material, just as sound thinking forces us to seek the cause of the advance of the hands of a clock in the laws of mechanics (the spirit of inorganic nature), not in a special demon who causes the movement of the hands. As a scientist, Ernst Haeckel justifiably had to reject the clumsy conception of a God thought of in the same way as something material. "In the higher and more abstract forms of religion this corporeal manifestation is abandoned, and God is worshipped only as *'pure spirit,'* without body. 'God is a spirit and he who worships Him must worship Him in spirit and in truth.' Nevertheless, the spiritual activity of this pure spirit is exactly the same as that of the anthropomorphous, divine personality. In reality this immaterial spirit too is not thought of as incorporeal, but as invisible, gaseous. We thus come to the paradoxical conception of God as a *gaseous vertebrate.*" (Haeckel, *Welträtsel*, The Riddle of the Universe, p. 333.) In reality, a sensory-factual existence of something spiritual can only be assumed where an immediate sensory experience shows the spiritual; and only that degree of the spiritual can be assumed which is perceived in this manner. The excellent thinker, B. Carneri, could say (in the work, *Empfindung und Bewusstsein,* Sensation and Consciousness, p. 15): "The sentence, No spirit without matter, but also no matter without spirit—would justify us in extending the problem also to plants, or even to the first rock we come across, where hardly anything could be said in favor of this correlation." Spiritual processes, as facts, are the results of different functions of an organism; the spirit of the world does not exist in the world in a material manner, but only in a spiritual manner. The soul of man is a sum of processes in which the spirit appears most immediately *as a fact.* But it is *only* in man that the spirit exists in the form of such a soul. And to seek the spirit in the form of a soul elsewhere than in man, to think of other beings as endowed with a soul like man, is to misunderstand the spirit; it is to commit the most grievous sin against the spirit. One who does this, only shows that he has not experienced the spirit itself within him; he has only experienced the external manifestation of the spirit that holds sway in him: that is, the soul. But this is just as if somebody were to mistake a circle drawn in pencil for the true mathematical-ideal circle. One who does not experience within himself anything but the soul-form of the spirit, feels impelled to assume such a soul-form also in non-human things, in order not to have to stop at gross sensory materiality. Instead of thinking of the primordial foundation of the world as spirit, he thinks of it as a world soul, and assumes a general animation of nature.

Giordano Bruno, under the impact of the new Copernican conception of nature, could grasp the spirit in the world, from which it had been expelled in its old form, only as a *world soul*. When one immerses oneself in Bruno's writings (especially in his profound book, *Of the Cause, the Principle, and the One*) one has the impression that he thought of things as being animated, although in different degrees. He has not in reality experienced the spirit within himself; therefore he imagines it in terms of the human soul, in which form alone it has confronted him. When he speaks of the spirit he understands it in this way. "The universal reason is the innermost, most real, and most characteristic faculty, and is a potential part of the world soul; it is something everywhere identical, which fills the All, illuminates the universe, and instructs nature in bringing forth its species as they should

be." It is true that in these sentences the spirit is not described as a "gaseous vertebrate," but as a being like the
human soul. "A thing however small and minute, has
within itself a portion of spiritual substance which, if it
finds the substratum to be suitable, strives to become
a plant or an animal, and organizes itself into a body of
some kind, which is generally called animated. For spirit
is to be found in all things, and there is not the most
minute body which does not contain such a portion of it
that it animates itself."—Because Giordano Bruno had not
really experienced the spirit as spirit within himself, he
could confuse the life of the spirit with the external me-
chanical functions by means of which Ramon Lull (1235-
1315), in his so-called *Great Art* had attempted to unveil
the mysteries of the spirit. A modern philosopher, Franz
Brentano, describes this *Great Art* as follows: "On con-
centric, individually turnable circular disks various concepts were inscribed, and then the most diverse combinations were produced by this means." What coincidence
superimposed upon a particular turn, was formed into a
judgment about the highest truths. And in his many wanderings about Europe, Giordano Bruno appeared at various universities as a teacher of this *Great Art*. He had the
boldness to think of the stars as worlds that are completely
analogous to our earth; he enlarged the vision of scientific
thinking beyond the earth; he no longer thought of the
heavenly bodies as *corporeal* spirits, but he still thought
of them as spirits of the *soul*. One must not do an injustice
to this man whom the Catholic church made to atone for
his advanced ideas with death. It was an enormous achieve-

ment to enfold the whole heavens in the same conception of the world that up to that time had been applied only to the things of the earth, even though Bruno still thought of the sensory as of something belonging to the soul.—

*

As a personality that made what Tauler, Weigel, Jacob Boehme and others had prepared shine once more in a great spiritual harmony, Johann Scheffler, called Angelus Silesius (1624-1677) appeared in the seventeenth century. The ideas of the above-mentioned thinkers appear in his book, *Cherubinischer Wandersmann, Geistreiche Sinn— und Schlussreime,* Cherubinic Wanderer, Ingenious Aphorisms in Rhymes, as though gathered in a spiritual focus and shining with a heightened luminosity. And everything Angelus Silesius utters appears as such an immediate, spontaneous revelation of his personality that it is as though this man had been destined by a special providence to embody wisdom in a personal form. The spontaneous way in which he lives his wisdom is shown by the fact that he expresses it in sayings which are also admirable for their artistic form. He floats above all earthly existence like a spiritual being, and what he utters is like the breath of another world, cleansed from the very beginning of all those coarse and impure elements from which human wisdom can free itself at other times only with difficulty.— In the sense of Angelus Silesius only he partakes of true cognition who makes the eye of the All to see within himself; only he sees his acts in their true light who feels them to be performed within himself by the hand of the All:

"God is the fire in me, and I the light in Him: do we not intimately belong to each other?"—"I am as rich as God; there is no grain of dust that I (Believe me, O Man) do not have in common with Him."—"God loves me above Himself; if I love Him above myself I give Him as much as He gives me out of Himself."—"The bird is in the air, the stone lies on the land; the fish lives in the water, my spirit in God's Hand."—"If you are born of God, then God blossoms in you; and His divinity is your sap and your ornament."—"Stop, whither are you running; Heaven is in you; if you seek God elsewhere you will forever miss Him."—For one who feels himself to exist in the All in this way, every separation between himself and another being ceases; he no longer feels himself to be a separate individual; on the contrary, he feels everything about himself to be a part of the world, while his true essence is identical with this universe itself. "The world does not hold you; you yourself are the world that, in you and with you, keeps you so strongly prisoner."—"Man does not have perfect bliss till the oneness has swallowed the otherness." —"Man is all things: if he lacks one, he himself truly does not know his wealth."—As a sensory being man is a thing among other things, and his sensory organs bring to him, as to a sensory individuality, sensory information about the things in space and time outside of him; but when the spirit speaks in man, then there is no outside and no inside; nothing that is spiritual is here and nothing is there; nothing is earlier, and nothing is later; space and time have disappeared in the contemplation of the universal spirit. It is only as long as man sees as an individual that he is here and the thing is there, and only as long as he sees as an individual, is this earlier and this later. "Man, if you let your spirit rise above place and time you can at every instant be in Eternity."—"I myself am Eternity when I leave time, and gather myself together in God, and God in myself."—"The rose which your external eye sees here, has bloomed like this in God through Eternity."— "Sit down in the center, and you shall see everything at once: what happens now and then, here and in Heaven."— "As long, my friend, as you have place and time in mind, you shall not grasp what God and Eternity are."—"When man withdraws from multiplicity and communes with God, he reaches unity."—With this the height has been climbed where man goes beyond his individual self and abolishes every contrast between the world and himself. A higher life begins for him. The inner experience which takes place in him appears to him like the death of the old life and a resurrection in the new. "When you raise yourself above yourself and let God act, then shall the Ascension take place in your spirit."—"The body must elevate itself in the spirit, the spirit in God, if you, O Man, wish to live in Him forever in bliss."—"As much as my I pines away and diminishes in me, so much is the Lord's I strengthened thereby."—It is from this point of view that man can understand his significance and the significance of all things in the realm of eternal necessity. The natural universe appears to him in a direct way as the divine spirit. The thought of a divine, universal spirit which could have its being and continuance above and beside the things of the world, fades away as a concept that has been surmounted. This universal spirit appears to be so poured out into things, to have become so much one nature with them, that it could not be imagined any longer if even a single part of its being were imagined as absent. "There is nothing but I and You; and if we two do not exist, then God is God no more, and the heavens shall fall."—Man feels himself to be a necessary link in the chain of the world. His acts no longer have any element of arbitrariness or individuality. What he does is necessary in the whole, in the chain of the world, which would fall apart if what he does were taken out of it. "Without me God cannot make a single worm; if I do not preserve it with Him, it must straightway fall to pieces."—"I know that without me God cannot live for an instant; if I come to nothing then He must needs give up the ghost."—It is only on this height that man sees things in their true nature. He no longer needs to attribute, from the outside, a spiritual essence to what is smallest, what is grossly sensory. For such as this smallest is, in all its smallness and gross, sensory nature, it is a part of the All. "No dust mote is so poor, no dot is so small, but the wise man sees God in it in His glory."—"In a mustard-seed, if you can understand it, is the image of all higher and lower things."—On this height man feels himself free. For coercion exists only where one can still be compelled by something from the outside. But when everything external has flowed into the interior, when the contrast between "I and world," outside and inside," "nature and spirit," has disappeared, then man feels everything which impels him only as his own impulse. "Fetter me as strictly as you want, in a thou-

sand irons; nevertheless I shall be wholly free and unfet-
tered."—"When *my* will is dead, then *must* God do what
I will; I myself prescribe to Him the pattern and the goal."
—Now all externally imposed moral norms cease to exist;
man becomes his own measure and goal. He is not subject
to any law, for the law too has become *his* nature. "The
law is for the wicked; if no commandment were written,
the godly would yet love God and their neighbor."—On
the higher level of cognition the *innocence of nature* is thus
given back to man. He accomplishes the tasks which are
set for him with the awareness of an eternal necessity. He
says to himself, Through this iron necessity is given into
your hand to withdraw that part which is assigned to you
from this same eternal necessity. "O Men, learn from the
flower of the field how you can please God and be beautiful at the same time."—"The rose is without why; it
blooms because it blooms; it pays no attention to itself,
nor asks whether one sees it."—When man arises to the
higher level he feels in himself the eternal and necessary
impulse of the universe, just as the flower of the field; he
acts as the flower blooms. In all his actions the awareness
of his moral responsibility grows into the immeasurable.
For what he does not do is withdrawn from the All, is a
killing of this All, insofar as the possibility of such a killing lies with him. "What is it not to sin? Do not ask much;
go, the silent flowers will tell you."—"Everything must
be slain. If you do not slay yourself for God, eternal death
shall at last slay you for the Enemy."

EPILOGUE

ALMOST TWO AND A HALF CENTURIES have passed since Angelus Silesius gathered together the profound wisdom of his precursors in his *Cherubinic Wanderer*. These centuries have brought rich insights into nature. Goethe opened a great perspective into natural science. He sought to pursue the eternal, iron laws of nature's action up to that peak where they bring forth man with the same inevitability with which, on a lower level, they produce a stone (cf. my book, *Goethes Weltanschauung*, Goethe's Conception of the World). Lamarck, Darwin, Haeckel and others have continued to work in the spirit of this way of thinking. The "question of all questions," that concerning the natural origin of man, was answered in the nineteenth century. Other problems in the realm of natural processes connected with this question, have been solved. Today one knows that one need not step outside the realm of the factual and sensory in order to understand, in a purely natural fashion, the sequence of beings in its development up to man.—And the nature of the human "I" too has been illuminated by the discernment of J. G. Fichte, which has shown the human soul where it should seek itself and what it is (cf. p. 106 above, and the section on Fichte in my book, *Welt—und Lebensanschauungen im neunzehnten Jahrhundert,* Conceptions of the World and of Life in the Nineteenth Century, published in a new edition as *Rätsel der Philosophie,* Riddles of Philosophy). Hegel has extended the domain of thought over all fields of being, and has endeavored to grasp in thought the external, sensory existence of nature as well as the highest creations of the human spirit, together with the laws by which they are governed (cf. my presentation of Hegel in *Rätsel der Philosophie,* v. 1).—How do the spirits, whose thoughts have been traced in this work, appear in the light of a conception of the world which takes into account the scientific achievements of the periods succeeding theirs? They still believe in a "supernatural" history of creation. How do their thoughts appear when confronted by the "natural" one which the science of the nineteenth century has developed?—This science has not given anything to nature which does not belong to it; it has only taken from it what does not belong to it. It has banished from it everything which is not to be sought in it, but is to be found only within man. It no longer sees something in nature that resembles the human soul and that acts in the same way as man. It no longer lets the forms of organisms be *created* by a manlike God; it traces their development in the world of the senses in accordance with purely natural laws. Meister Eckhart as well as Tauler, and Jacob Boehme as well as Angelus Silesius, would needs feel the most profound satisfaction in the contemplation of this natural science. The spirit in which *they* wished to regard the world has passed in the fullest sense into this conception of nature *when it is properly understood*. What they could not yet do, that is, to place the facts of nature into that light which had arisen in them, would no doubt have become their desire if this natural science had been accessible to them. They could not do this, for no geology, no "natural history of creation" told them of the processes of nature. The Bible alone, in its own way, told them of such processes. Therefore, as well as they could, they sought the spiritual where alone it is to be found: within the human being. Today they would employ quite different resources than at their time in order to show that, in a form accessible to the senses, the spirit is only to be found in man. Today they would entirely agree with those who seek the spirit as fact, not at the root of nature, but in its fruit. They would admit that the spirit in the sensory body is the *result of development,* and that such a spirit cannot be sought on lower levels of development. They would understand that no "creative thought" was active in the formation of the spirit in the organism, any more than such a "creative thought" made the ape develop out of the marsupials.— Our present time cannot speak about the facts of nature in the same way as Jacob Boehme spoke about them. But today also there is a point of view which brings the way of thinking of Jacob Boehme close to a conception of the world that takes account of modern science. One need not lose the spirit when one finds in nature only what is natural. It is true that today there are many who think that

234 Mysticism at the Dawn of the Modern Age

one must slip into a shallow, dry materialism if one accepts the "facts" discovered by natural science without
further ado. I myself stand completely upon the ground
of this natural science. I have the definite conviction that
with a conception of nature such as that of Ernst Haeckel,
only he can become shallow who approaches it with a
world of ideas that is already shallow. I feel something
higher and more glorious when I let the *revelations* of the
"natural history of creation" act upon me than when I am
confronted with the stories of supernatural miracles of
the Creed. I know of nothing in any "holy" book that reveals to me anything as sublime as the "dry" fact that, in
the womb, every human fetus rapidly goes through a succession of all those forms through which its animal ancestors have evolved. Let us fill our mind with the magnifi-
cence of the facts our senses perceive, and we shall care
little for the "miracles" which do not lie within the course
of nature. If we experience the spirit within ourselves we
do not require one in external nature. In my *Philosophie
der Freiheit* I have described my conception of the world,
which does not think that it is driving out the spirit because it regards nature in the same way as do Darwin and
Haeckel. A plant, an animal, do not gain anything for me
if I people them with souls of which my senses tell me
nothing. I do not seek a "deeper," "spiritual" nature of
things in the external world, I do not even assume it, because I believe that the cognition which illuminates my
inner self preserves me from doing so. I believe that the
things of the sensory world are what they appear to us
to be, for I see that a true self-knowledge leads us to seek

in nature nothing but natural processes. I seek no divine spirit in nature, because I believe that I perceive the essence of the human spirit in myself. I calmly acknowledge my animal ancestors, because I believe I understand that where these animal ancestors have their origin, no soul-like spirit *can be active.* I can only agree with Ernst Haeckel when he prefers "the eternal stillness of the grave" to such an immortality as many a religion teaches (cf. Haeckel's *Welträtsel,* The Riddle of the Universe, p. 239). For I find a degradation of the spirit, a repugnant sin *against the spirit,* in the conception of a soul which continues to exist after the fashion of a sensory being.—I hear a shrill dissonance when the facts of natural science in Haeckel's presentation encounter the "piety" of the creeds of many contemporaries. But in creeds which are in but poor harmony with natural facts, there resounds for me nothing of the spirit of the higher piety which I find in Jacob Boehme and Angelus Silesius. This higher piety is rather in full harmony with the action of the natural. There is no contradiction in becoming penetrated with the insights of modern science and at the same time in entering upon the road which Jacob Boehme and Angelus Silesius pursued in their search for the spirit. One who enters upon this road in the spirit of these thinkers need not fear that he will slip into shallow materialism if he lets the secrets of nature be described to him by a "natural history of creation." One who interprets my ideas in this sense will understand in the same way as I the last saying of the *Cherubinic Wanderer,* which shall also sound the last note of this work: "Friend, it is enough now. If you wish to read more, go and become yourself the writing and the essence."

* * *

[Footnote added to the 1923 edition: The last sentences above must not be misinterpreted as expressing an *unspiritual* conception of nature. Through them I only wanted to emphasize strongly that the spirit which lies at the root of nature must be found *in* it, and is not to be brought into it from the outside. The rejection of "creative thoughts" refers to an activity which is similar to human activity, and proceeds according to ideas of usefulness. What is to be said about evolutionary history one may find in my book, *Erkenntnistheorie der Goetheschen Weltanschauung*, The Theory of Knowledge in Goethe's Conception of the World, preface to the new edition.]

ADDENDA TO THE 1923 EDITION

Addendum I (p. 126). The fear of an impoverishment of the life of the soul through an ascent to the spirit is to be found only in those personalities that know the spirit only in a sum of concepts abstracted from sensory perceptions. One who in spiritual seeing raises himself to a life that surpasses the life of the senses in content and in concreteness, cannot know this fear. For it is only in abstractions that the sensory existence grows pale; in the "spiritual seeing," for the first time it appears in its true light, without losing anything of its sensory richness.

Addendum II (p. 165). In my writings, "mysticism" is spoken of in different ways. The *apparent* contradiction which some persons have claimed to find in this is elucidated in the annotations to the new edition of my *Erkenntnistheorie der Goetheschen Weltanschauung,* The Theory of Knowledge in Goethe's Conception of the World.

Addendum III (p. 188). In a few words I hint here at the road to the cognition of the spirit which I have described in my later writings, especially in *Wie erlangt man Erkenntnisse der höheren Welten,* How does one Attain Knowledge of the Higher Worlds, *Umriss einer Geheimwissenschaft,* Outline of a Secret Science, *Von Seelenrätseln,* Riddles of the Soul.

PREFACE TO THE FIRST EDITION, 1901

WHAT I DISCUSS in this work previously formed the content of lectures which I gave in the course of the past winter at the theosophical library in Berlin. I had been invited by Count and Countess Brockdorff to talk on mysticism before an audience to whom the things dealt with in this connection are a vital question of great importance.—Ten years ago I would not yet have dared to comply with such a wish. This must not be taken to mean that the world of ideas to which I give expression today was not alive in me at that time. This world of ideas is already wholly contained in my *Philosophie der Freiheit*, Philosophy of Spiritual Activity, (Berlin, 1894). But in order *so* to express this world of ideas as I do today, and thus to make it the basis of a discussion as is done in this work, something is needed in addition to an unshakeable conviction of its conceptual truth. This requires an intimate familiarity with this world of ideas, such as can only be attained in the course of many years of one's life. Only now, after I have acquired this familiarity, do I dare to speak in the way which one will discover in this work.

He who does not encounter my world of ideas with an *open mind* will discover contradiction upon contradiction in it. Only recently have I dedicated a book on the philosophies of the nineteenth century (Berlin, 1900) to the great scientist Ernst Haeckel, a book which I terminated with a justification of his ideas. In the following expositions I speak with assenting devotion about the mystics from Meister Eckhart to Angelus Silesius. Of other "contradictions" which someone or other might enumerate, I shall not speak at all.—I am not surprised if I am condemned by one side as a "mystic," by the other as a "materialist."— If I find that the Jesuit priest Müller has solved a difficult chemical problem, and if I therefore agree with him without reservations *in this matter,* one can hardly condemn me as an adherent of Jesuitism without being considered a fool by the judicious.

One who like myself goes his own way is bound to be exposed to many misunderstandings. But fundamentally he can bear this easily. Such misunderstandings are generally self-evident for him when he considers the mental make-up of his critics. It is not without humorous feelings that I look back upon many a "critical" judgment I have received in the course of my career as a writer. At the beginning everything went well. I wrote about Goethe and in connection with him. What I said sounded to many as though they could fit it into their preconceived notions. This was done by saying, "A work such as Rudolf Steiner's introductions to the scientific writings of Goethe can be described honestly as the best that has been written on this question." When later I published an independent work

I had already become much more stupid. For now a benevolent critic gave the following advice: "Before he continues to reform and brings his *Philosophy of Spiritual Activity* into the world, one must urgently advise him first to penetrate to an understanding of those two philosophers (Hume and Kant)." The critic unfortunately knows only what he can manage to read in Kant and Hume; thus he really only advises me to see nothing in these thinkers beyond what he sees. When I shall have achieved this he will be satisfied with me.—When my *Philosophie der Freiheit* appeared I was in need of being judged like the most ignorant beginner. This judgment I received from a gentleman whom hardly anything forces to write books except the fact that there are innumerable volumes by others— which he has not understood. He informs me with much thoughtfulness that I would have noticed my mistakes if I "had pursued deeper psychological, logical, and epistemological studies;" and he immediately enumerates for me all the books which I should read in order to become as clever as he: "Mill, Sigwart, Wundt, Riehl, Paulsen, B. Erdmann."—Especially diverting for me was the advice of a man who is so impressed by the way he "understands" Kant that he cannot even imagine someone's having *read* Kant and nevertheless having an opinion different from his. He therefore indicates to me the chapters in question in Kant's writings from which I might acquire an understanding of Kant as profound as his own.

I have here adduced a few *typical* judgments concerning my world of ideas. Although they are insignificant in themselves they appear to me to be well suited to indicate symptomatically certain facts which today constitute serious obstacles in the path of one who writes on questions of higher cognition. I must go my way, no matter whether one gives me the good advice to read Kant, or whether another accuses me of heresy because I agree with Haeckel. And so I have written about mysticism without caring what the judgments of a credulous materialist may be. I would only like—so that no printer's ink is quite needlessly wasted—to inform those who may now perhaps advise me to read Haeckel's *Welträtsel, The Riddle of the Universe,* that in the last months I have given about thirty lectures on this book.

I hope to have shown in my work that one can be a faithful follower of the scientific philosophy and still seek out the paths *to the soul* into which mysticism, *properly understood,* leads. I go even further and affirm: Only one who understands the spirit in the sense of *true* mysticism can attain a full understanding of facts in the realm of nature. One must only beware of confusing true mysticism with the "mysticism" of muddled heads. How mysticism can err I have shown in my *Philosophie der Freiheit.*

Berlin, September 1901

RUDOLF STEINER

INDEX